D1253030

The
Charity
Racket

Also by Robert A. Liston

The Charity Racket

by
Robert A. Liston

THOMAS NELSON INC., PUBLISHERS
Nashville / New York

First edition

Library of Congress Cataloging in Publication Data

Liston, Robert A
    The charity racket.

    Includes index.
    1. Charities—United States. 2. Fund raising—United States.
I. Title.
HV91.L57   1976   361.7'0973   76–43081
    ISBN 0–8407–6512–6

Contents

The
Charity
Racket

Introduction

It is difficult, sometimes impossible, to obtain meaningful information on the manner in which charities raise their money, or to find out what they do with it after they get it. That may be why there aren't many books on the subject of charities.

One can think of several reasons for it. Americans consider giving to be a private act, the public displays of generosity on telethons being an exception. People do not want their giving to be known or reported. Income-tax forms, which list charity contributions, are confidential. Gifts, including church offerings, are sealed in envelopes.

Furthermore, the charities who receive all this personal, secret money apparently believe that the donors' privacy applies to them too, although there is no reason why it should. At any rate, most charities vigorously defend themselves against any "outside" snooping into their financial affairs.

INTRODUCTION

That is unfortunate, because the secrecy gives the impression that the charities have something to hide. Some of them, at least, do, as the pages to come will reveal.

In any event, the reader's forbearance is asked in the matter of statistics. I have had to use the phrase "a recent year" when giving figures. Generally these figures are for the years 1971 through 1974. Unfortunately, certain figures were available for one of those years, but not for another, so I have avoided the use of years to avoid confusion. In any case, the figures are intended to be relative and illustrative, not definitive.

I am not against charity, far from it. I am not recommending any particular charity as better than another, and I am not, except in obvious instances of rackets, trying to make a particular charity look bad. I am not motivated by malice, and have no particular charitable ax to grind. I have described many charities, but the reader will surely understand that only a fraction of our tens of thousands of philanthropic organizations can be mentioned.

I am indebted to many people. I would like to single out those individuals who assisted with the research: Mrs. Eleanor R. Seagraves of Washington, D.C., Mr. David O. Strickland and Mr. Dennis K. Warner, both of New York City, and Mrs. Betty Peterzell of Stamford, Connecticut. All of these good friends were of invaluable aid. My wife Jean and daughter Felicia assisted with the manuscript.

—R.A.L.

1

The American Way
of Giving

Americans may be the most generous people on earth. We are always giving away money—a check in the mail, a dollar or two at the door, a few coins in collection boxes. We have it deducted from our wages. We bequeath money or property to charity upon our deaths. We give of our time—most generously. It is said more than 40 million Americans perform volunteer charity work each year.

In the name of charity, we buy Girl Scout cookies—66 million boxes in a recent year—candy from Campfire Girls, paper poppies, Christmas Seals, Easter Seals, pamphlets, books, magazines, ident-o-tags, greeting cards, ballpoint pens, candles and much, much more.

The biggest share of our giving—over $10 billion in a recent year—goes for religion. We give our money to Protestant, Catholic, and Jewish churches and synagogues, to the Jehovah's Witnesses, the Assembly of God, the Children of God, the Zen Buddhists, the Hare Khrishnas, and even to The Holy Spirit Association for the Unification of World Christianity.

That same year we gave almost $4 billion to colleges and universities and other educational institutions, and this was in addition to tuition and fees paid by students. We gave another $4 billion to support hospitals and to efforts to eradicate diseases such as cancer, heart disease, arthritis, lung disease, kidney disease, leukemia, cystic fibrosis, multiple sclerosis, muscular dystrophy, hemophilia, epilepsy, and asthma. We also regularly give to help the blind, the deaf, the crippled, the mentally ill, and the retarded.

Our purse seems bottomless. We give to the poor, hungry, and needy, the unemployed, the sick, the elderly, the orphaned, and the divorced. We give to the Boy Scouts, the Boys' Clubs of America, the YMCA and YWCA, to the Little League, the America the Beautiful Fund, to Voices in Vital America, to Help Hospitalized Veterans, to the Disabled American Veterans, to Stop Immorality on TV, to the Dokota Indian Foundation, to Americans Against Union Control of Government, to the Wisdom Society, to the National Police Officers' Association of America, to Ann Adams Greetings, to Futures for Children, to Friends of Animals, to University Professors for Academic Order, to the Unstoppables, to Welcome Home P.O.W., to Project Lifeguard, and to Citizens for Decent Literature—a few among many thousands.

Nor is our charity limited to the United States. We give to the American Red Cross, which aids American servicemen overseas, performs disaster relief, and collects blood for use worldwide. We give to the USO and to CARE, the United Israel Appeal, the American-Korean Foundation, the Christian Children's Fund, the Foster Parents' Plan, the Holt Adoption Program, the Save The

Children Federation, as well as to the American Bureau for Medical Aid to China, the American Foundation for Overseas Blind, the American Jewish Joint Distribution Committee, the Catholic Relief Services, the International Rescue Committee, the United Hias Service, and the Meals for Millions Foundation—a few of many organizations collecting money in America to help the unfortunate in other lands.

We also give the United Way.

The total of all this giving in 1975 was $29 billion. In 1974, it was $25.15 billion. As computed by the American Association of Fund-Raising Counsel, Inc., an organization of professional fund-raising firms, this giving by Americans broke down this way:

Type of Giving	In Billions	% of Total
Religion	$10.85	43.1
Health and Hospitals	3.90	15.5
Education	3.72	14.8
Social Welfare	2.34	9.3
Arts and Humanities	1.28	5.1
Civic and Public	.71	2.8
Other, including foundation endowment, foreign aid, and international affairs	2.35	9.4
Total	$25.15	100.0%

Who gave this stupendous sum to charity? According to the same organization, 4.7 percent came from business corporations and 8.4 percent from foundations; 8.2 percent was left in bequests by the deceased, and 78.7 percent was contributed by individuals in acts of personal generosity. All of this money was disbursed to more than a half million organizations, agencies, and causes.

15

As gigantic as these figures are, they do not begin to measure the amount of giving in America. The $29 billion does not include the income that comes from past gifts. Americans have been giving for over 200 years. Churches, synagogues, other religious bodies, colleges, universities, hospitals, museums, libraries, and other institutions and organizations have received sums that now total hundreds of billions of dollars. These endowments are invested in stocks, bonds, other securities, land, buildings, and business enterprises that produce billions of dollars a year in income. We have figures for just a small part of this endowment income.

Since 1911, wealthy Americans have been setting up foundations such as the Ford Foundation and the Rockefeller Foundation to carry on various types of philanthropy after the donor's death. More than 25,000 foundations have been created, and they control assets of well over $34 billion. These foundations spent over $2 billion on charity in a recent year.

Also, giving in America must include the innumerable acts of unrecorded individual charity and the countless raffles, bingo games, bake sales, rummage sales, car washings, membership drives, and other activities by which church, educational, civic, service, and fraternal clubs and organizations raise money for charity. A group may raise only a few dollars for charity through a bazaar or stage show, but we must conclude that when such activities are repeated millions of times a year all over the nation, the total amount of money is both large and unknown.*

*This book is about private charity. Some mention should be made, however, of the many tens of billions of tax dollars spent by federal, state, and local governments each year for the same purposes as private charity—to care for the young, old, sick, and handicapped. Unemploy-

THE AMERICAN WAY OF GIVING

Why do Americans give so much? There are probably as many reasons for giving as there are people to give. Some give, surely, because of sympathy for the plight of the sick and needy. Religious teachings encourage the belief that gifts are a form of offering to a deity. Also, people like to help an institution or organization because they feel its purposes and activities are worthwhile, or they may believe that if they help others, they will be helped in return. Feeling thankful for one's blessings can create a desire to share with others, as can guilt over past actions or over the manner in which money was accumulated. Other reasons for giving are the desire to escape taxes, which is the same as making money by giving a little of it to charity.

Among the reasons for giving to charity is the desire to think of ourselves as generous and to have others believe we are generous, or at least not niggardly. Generosity is a highly prized human trait. We honor thrift, yet stinginess is a most unwanted and ridiculed attribute. We Americans (other nationalities, too) engage in various rituals to avoid any appearance of being tightwads. Grown men compete to buy each other drinks in a bar or to pick up the check in a restaurant or to be the quickest to buy tickets at a theater. Women keep track of who invited whom to parties, what type of affair it was, and what was served. An effort is made to reciprocate with a similar invitation. We count our Christmas cards and keep a list of those who sent us one. No one wants to appear ungenerous. Con-

ment compensation, public welfare, and social security are but three tax-supported programs that might be considered acts of indirect charity. Public appropriations also go for education, health care, medical research, and other programs supported by private charity. Foreign aid alone has claimed more than $140 billion in American tax money since World War II.

versely, a cardinal social sin is to put people in the position of appearing ungenerous when they are not.

Generosity, giving, people helping people—these virtues have always been of special importance in the United States. The nature of our founding made it so. Most of our early colonists were deeply religious people and therefore were committed to charity through their teachings. These men settled a virgin land where the climate was often harsh. The land, the climate, and sometimes unfriendly Indians made life hard for the settlers. To survive, they were forced to cooperate—to help one another in building shelter, tilling the soil, by sharing food, and in self-defense. This pattern was repeated as Americans moved westward to a succession of frontiers. Community house and barn raisings, planting, harvesting, and defense became traditions. Neighbor helped neighbor in times of sickness, hunger, or disaster. These customs have not disappeared in America, but have been strengthened with time.*

The American attitude toward charity was also formed by the absence of feudalism and an established church. In the feudal societies of the Middle Ages in Europe, the mass of the people were serfs, who farmed the land or worked for the land-owning nobility, who, in turn, provided food, shelter, and protection. Serfs lived at little more than the subsistence level. The whole organization of society, including charity, came either from the nobility or the Catholic Church, the established or state religion of the time. Such concepts as self-help, self-im-

---

*Lest this be doubted, consider the actions of Americans during many recent floods, storms, and other disasters. Total strangers come to each other's aid, often performing acts of heroism and self-sacrifice. Even the supposedly callous New Yorkers reacted with friendliness and charity during the famous power blackout in 1965.

provement, neighbor helping neighbor were difficult to practice.

The Renaissance, which marked the end of the Middle Ages, came to Europe a full century and more before the American colonies were settled. Attempts were made to plant the seeds of a nobility and an established church in America, but these ideas would not take root. The closest America came to a feudal society was in the large plantations of the South, where slavery was practiced. The middle and northern colonies were almost entirely settled by small farmers and shopkeepers, all independent and self-reliant. There was little place for a nobility or a state religion, and thus charity came to be an individual act of neighborliness and compassion. It ceased to be the province of the aristocracy and the Church.

The concept of charity as an individual act of generosity received great impetus from the industrialists and financiers who founded the great American corporations in the decades just before and after the turn of this century. During their lifetimes, and ever since, many of these men were called "robber barons." The term had some accuracy, for in building their industrial and financial empires, these men did truly rob—the land, its resources, the people, and even each other.

They engaged in the most cutthroat forms of competition, snuffing out and absorbing many businessmen whose only failure was in not being big enough or rich enough to compete with them. They often made shoddy merchandise and then raised the prices on it. They repeatedly overproduced in a lust for money and power, and then thrust the nation into one economic depression after another. They frequently bribed mayors, governors, even cabinet officers, judges, and legislators, until they practically *were* government in many places in the United

States. They tried to stop any interference in their affairs, and, time after time, perhaps hundreds of times, they sacrificed their own workers by the dozen and by the score in the name of free enterprise.

The robber barons made American industrially and financially the most powerful nation on earth. They built the railroads and the factories, drilled the oil wells and opened the mines, cut the timber, strung the nation with electrical wire, and crisscrossed it with highways. Our great banking institutions were founded by them. Strangely, rather few of our large modern corporations today bear the names of the robber barons who founded and labored so hard for them. There are the names of Ford in motor vehicles, Kellogg in cereal, Du Pont in chemicals, Mellon in banking, and a few others.

Most of the robber barons have had their names immortalized in their philanthropies—Rockefeller Center, Rockefeller University, Carnegie-Mellon University, Stanford University, Duke University, Vanderbilt University, Henry Ford Hospital, as well as in many libraries, museums, and cultural centers that were named for their principal benefactors. Like the old feudal nobility, Americans of gigantic wealth believed in philanthropy, practiced it during their lifetimes,* and upon their death gave vast sums to various charities. They endowed existing institutions and frequently set up new ones. They created foundations bearing their names to perpetuate charitable exercises in their name. They

*A famous example was the practice of John D. Rockefeller, Sr., the founder of the family fortune and the grandfather of Nelson A. Rockefeller, of doling out his oil profits a nickel at a time to children. He later raised it to a dime when inflation set in. Rockefeller also gave large sums of money to charity during his lifetime, as did his son, John D. Rockefeller, Jr., his grandchildren, and his great-grandchildren.

filled library shelves with the books they had collected and graced museums with the art and artifacts they had accumulated. The widows and children and grandchildren of these fantastically wealthy men also gave away, upon their deaths, much of the money they had inherited.

We can only speculate what motives the very wealthy have for giving to charity. Some were and are doubtlessly motivated by genuine compassion toward others. A few may be seeking memorials to their names, still others may be attempting to assuage a sense of guilt for the manner in which the money was obtained or for the fact of being rich. Another motive, which we will consider in detail a little later, may be a desire to keep the fortune intact and even control it from the grave. Establishing a foundation is an important way to avoid the payment of estate or inheritance taxes, as well as to govern how the money is to be spent for generations to come. Whatever the motives of wealthy philanthropists, it is certain that giving to charity is a long-established practice among them.

Religious groups in the United States have long been involved in organized charity. Members of churches, synagogues, and other religious organizations care for the ill and needy in their congregations. They raise money for missions and for disbursement among needy families, and they also carry on a variety of educational, social, and medical philanthropies.

It has virtually disappeared today, but for a long time the principal nonreligious form of charity in the United States was carried on by the political machines. Political bosses, particularly in big cities, were in the business of gaining votes, winning elections, and controlling governmental power, and their purpose in helping the needy may have been anything but charitable. However, the effect of their activities was similar to that of organized charity.

Between about 1870 and 1920, millions of immigrants arrived in the United States. They came looking for freedom, with the expectation of finding greater wealth and improved social conditions. What many, perhaps most, found at first was a despicable slum in an American city. The worst slums or ghettos in America today, the South Bronx in New York, Roxbury in Boston, for example, do not begin to rival the urban slums of the turn of the century. They were warrens of firetrap tenements, full of poverty, disease, filth, infestations, and hopelessness. Many were simply European ghettos transported to America—language, customs, and all.

In a search for political loyalties and votes, the political bosses of the era—largely of the Democratic party—performed a needed social function. Their political clubs offered some basis of organization to the immigrant groups. They provided leadership, broke down language barriers, introduced immigrants to American ways, and offered jobs, if only political ones, to the young and enterprising. The political bosses doled out bags of coal and baskets of food and aided people in trouble with the law. Again, the purpose of these acts was political power, but the deeds were similar to those performed by thousands of better motivated charities today.

The "charity" of the political bosses lasted until the 1930s, when many of their functions were taken over by the government in the form of public welfare, unemployment compensation, and social security. The political boss today still seeks to cement loyalty by doing favors, but his activities are more on the order of fixing traffic tickets, having snow removed from a street, assigning a policeman to direct traffic at a charity bazaar, and arranging for the mayor to attend a social gathering.

Organized, nonsectarian charities as we know them today began to be formed in the late 1800s. Women were in the forefront of the movement. Jane Addams went into the infested Chicago slums and founded Hull House so she could give poor, immigrant children a chance to better themselves. Lillian Wald, a nurse, provided a similar service to the poor with the Henry Street Settlement in New York. The Salvation Army, which originated in England, came to the United States in 1880. Dorothea Dix carried on a crusade for more humane treatment of the mentally ill. Dr. Benjamin Blick founded the Pennsylvania Society for the Prevention of Tuberculosis and thereby began the voluntary health charity movement in America.

But when Clara Barton founded the American Red Cross, she began the movement toward nationally organized charities. Her story is a familiar one. During the Civil War she became an "angel of mercy," often caring for the wounded and dying singlehanded. In an era when wounded soldiers were often abandoned to die of minor wounds or sent to vermin-infested "hospitals" to die of filth and neglect, Clara Barton went from battlefield to battlefield trying to bathe, treat, and comfort as many of the wounded as she could. She set up soup kitchens and in many other ways sought to aid and solace the men at the front. Her activities became legendary. She become a symbol of womanly mercy amid the bestiality of war.

When the conflict ended, Clara Barton set out to establish a civilian hospital corps so that in the future wars, American fighting men would receive better medical treatment. She encountered a great deal of personal ridicule and public apathy, but she pursued her goal until the American Red Cross was established in 1881 as a national organization of volunteers who raised money from private sources to carry on charitable work. She was determined to make the American Red Cross not only valuable, but respected. She deliberately sought to enlist the aid and support of well-to-do, well-thought-of members of the community and to win recognition from the United States government. Her efforts were rewarded in 1900 when her organization received a congressional charter to carry on its work. Ridicule and apathy toward the organization finally ended in 1917, when Red Cross officers and nurses went overseas with American servicemen in World War I and performed heroic tasks on behalf of the wounded.

Today the Red Cross has over 36 million members. Although the military services now have their own medical corps, the Red Cross performs important liaison tasks for the armed forces by acting as a link between servicemen and their families.* Other workers act as hospital auxiliaries and provide comfort for the wounded. The Red Cross also provides disaster-relief services at home and abroad and operates a major blood-donor program, among other activities.

An important milestone in the growth of organized charity in the United States was the election of Franklin D. Roosevelt as President in 1932. The nation was mired in the Great Depression, the longest and one of the worst in history. Roosevelt called his administration's program the New Deal and said it would remember the "forgotten man." In his actions as President and in his radio addres-

---

*When I was in the Army in Korea in 1953, reports on the illness and death of my mother were brought to me by a Red Cross man.

ses to the nation called fireside chats, FDR awakened the nation's sense of social consciousness about the plight of the poor, the sick, the needy, and the handicapped, and in the 1930s, with a quarter of the work force jobless, that included a great many people. Dozens of governmental programs were started to get people back to work and to ease the suffering of millions.

Roosevelt's greatest gift to organized charity evolved from the fact that he himself was a cripple. He had been stuck down by polio in the prime of life, but had lived and regained his health. When he was elected President, he was confined to a wheelchair and could stand and walk only on crutches, but with his jaunty smile and vigorous wave, he became a symbol of courage and of the possibility that any American could surmount obstacles and rise to the highest office in the land.

FDR made polio his personal charity. His goal was to provide help for those afflicted with the disease and to find a way to cure or prevent it if possible. In 1938, he announced the formation of the National Foundation for Infantile Paralysis (as polio was called in those days) and appointed his good friend Basil O'Connor as its president. The board of directors, most of whom were FDR's friends, read like a miniature version of *Who's Who in America*.

Under O'Connor's leadership, the National Foundation became the nation's leading national charity. He organized the March of Dimes, centered around FDR's birthday, January 30, and urged Americans to join the fight against polio, if only with a dime. He started a new era in fund raising by enlisting the support of movie and radio celebrities and launching a massive campaign over radio on behalf of the charity. Although the disease afflicted adults as well as children, O'Connor portrayed it as a childhood disease and plucked the nation's heartstrings with photos of beautiful smiling children in leg braces hobbling on crutches. Although the incidence of polio was never particularly high, certainly far less than many other diseases, O'Connor labeled it a scourge and a pestilence and warned of epidemics—in short he scared American parents out of their wits.

In the first campaign in 1938, the March of Dimes raised $1.8 million, a huge sum for those days. During the next 20 years, the National Foundation averaged $30 million a year from its drive. In that time, the National Foundation spent $550 million for the conquest of polio—and it won with the development of the Salk polio vaccine in 1953. Five years later the Salk vaccine was in widespread use, and almost overnight, polio was stricken from the list of dread diseases afflicting mankind.

O'Connor had shown the way to make the charity dollars pour in. He also "proved" to the American people that if they gave enough money and if enough of it was spent for research, all the ills and problems of mankind could be eliminated. We conquered polio with dimes, didn't we?

The result has been a tremendous proliferation in the number of charities and charitable causes, as well as a vast increase in the amount raised through giving. Twenty-nine billion dollars. Charity is big business in America.

2

The Business of Charity

At precisely 10:07 A.M. on February 4, 1974, in Room 4232 of the Dirksen Senate Office Building in Washington, Senator Walter F. Mondale, Democrat of Minnesota, gaveled to order his Subcommittee on Children and Youth of the Committee on Labor and Public Welfare. Senator Mondale, who in 1976 was elected United States Vice President, and his compatriot, Senator William D. Hathaway, Democrat of Maine, and the only other senator present, were beginning a series of important hearings on how well or poorly children's charities serve both children and the public who contributes.

The first witness was a strange one for such important hearings. He was the national chairman of the National Easter Seal Society, which raises more than $37 million a year on behalf of crippled children. What was odd was that the witness was actor Peter Falk, better known perhaps for his role as the detective Colombo in a television series. One might have expected the national chairman of the Easter Seal Society to be a distinguished orthopedic specialist or neurosurgeon or some other expert in the field, or even a handicapped person who had overcome his difficulties to rise to prominence in American life. Peter Falk has only one eye, but that hardly qualifies him as an expert on crippled children.

It has become standard practice for a charity to have a movie or television celebrity as its national chairperson. In 1974 the American Cancer Society, the largest of the health charities, raised over $73 million from contributions, and that year its national chairperson was the actress Raquel Welch. Ms. Welch has made many movies and is certainly a celebrity, but in her career she is better known for her contours and for being a sex symbol than for her acting ability. Many people, notably members of the press, found it hard to take her seriously as national chairperson of the country's leading medical charity. At her introduction as chairperson at a press conference, Ms. Welch was reportedly both angered and tearful when smirking reporters questioned her facetiously. She was particularly annoyed when they asked her what qualifications she possessed to head the American Cancer Society.

Mr. Falk fared better with the Senate subcommittee. Prior to the hearing, he breakfasted with the senators, and he was treated with deference and respect during his brief appearance. Senator Hathaway even asked him jokingly if he would be more comfortable smoking a cigar and wearing a rumpled raincoat, a reference to Mr. Falk's paraphernalia for his TV show.

Mr. Falk's testimony was frank. He admitted that he knew very little about the medical causes for childhood handicaps and, that indeed, he knew very little about the Easter Seal Society. He had become interested in the plight of crippled children, he said, while appearing on a national telethon to raise funds for the charity. He had come for a few minutes and had stayed hours and had thereafter done as much work as he could with crippled children, whose courage and spirit he admired. When asked to become national chairman, he had accepted. In his prepared statement, Mr. Falk appealed for greater thoughtfulness toward handicapped persons. He described the difficulties many have in obtaining jobs, riding on buses or subways, and even using a pay phone, particularly if they are in a wheelchair.

The two senators were gentle in their questioning of Mr. Falk, much more so than they were to be with many later witnesses. Most of the newspaper headlines were derived from Mr. Falk's testimony that actors and actresses accept charity chairmanships and similar posts "mostly on faith." They really do not know whether the charity is efficiently run, how it raises its money, or if the funds are spent for the purposes for which they were given.

Senator Hathaway asked Mr. Falk if he had made any investigation of the Easter Seal program before agreeing to become national chairman. Mr. Falk replied that he had hosted two telethons and talked to enough handicapped people to "get some idea" of where the money went. Then he added:

"I would say that that would not have been a bad idea if, prior to my being asked to be national chairman, they had insisted that I go around and see more of their organization. Maybe they were anxious to have me and they did not care."

He also spoke frankly about his role as a contributor to charities and perhaps thereby expressed the feelings of many people:

"I know I am bombarded, as a lot of people are, with requests for donations, and you have no way of judging it. You get it in the mail. You do not know whether the organization is any good or not. You do not know where the money is going. You do not know what is happening. It is becoming increasingly popular among people to read all of this literature with a somewhat cynical response. Somewhere, some part of you is saying you are not quite sure what is happening. I think that decreases the power of these appeals."

If the national chairman of an important charity makes such a statement, what then are the millions of contributors to think when their only knowledge of the charity is the appeal they receive in the mail?

If Mr. Falk and all other contributors were to make a tour of charity organizations, they would find they resemble any other business with a comparable revenue. There are no factories and warehouses, to be sure, because charities do not produce a material product, but they do have a national headquarters and many branch offices, frequently called chapters. In that regard, charity resembles the type of profit-making organization that provides a service, such as an advertising agency, a public-relations firm, a large law office, or a consulting organization.

Like any other corporation, a charity has a chairman, frequently an honorary one such as Mr. Falk or Ms. Welch. The board of directors usually consists of prominent medical experts in the health field, bankers, educators, public officials, large donors and experts in various fields. The board members may provide expert opinion on various matters pertaining to the charity, but like the chairman, they are usually unpaid volunteers, although they may be reimbursed for their expenses when they attend the infrequent board meetings.

THE BUSINESS OF CHARITY

The day-to-day operations of the organization are handled by a staff usually headed by a person bearing a title such as president, executive vice president, or executive secretary. He is most likely to be a person with experience both in fund raising and in management. He (occasionally she) is well paid, with a salary of $25,000 a year and up, plus expenses. Among the highest paid is Paul E. Funk, executive vice president of the Epilepsy Foundation of America. In a recent year, his salary was just under $42,000 a year. He has twice signed a two-year employment contract, and was given a $12,000 bonus each time for signing. The Foundation also provided him with a new car for his personal use, first a Buick Rivera, then an AMX sports car. Both cars were leased for him.

Usually the headquarters staff of a charity organization is divided into functional areas much as a corporation would be. It will have a business office or accounting section, which usually has data-processing equipment to help it keep track of receipts and expenditures; a legal staff; advertising and public-relations departments; personnel officers; and so on.

Charities also have major departments appropriate to the functions of the organization. There are fund-raising departments, public-education departments to keep people informed of the charity and its work, and community-service departments, which work with local chapters and others involved locally in the charitable cause. In the case of a health charity, there will also be a patient-care section to supervise activities in hospitals and like facilities, and a research department, which will supervise the issuance of grants to universities, hospitals, and other institutions studying the charity's particular disease or ailment.

Other charities are organized differently. The Red

Cross, for example, is divided according to its various programs, such as blood donation, disaster relief, military, and drug abuse. The Girl Scouts and Boy Scouts have national organizations, but most of the power resides with largely autonomous regional councils, which supervise troop activity, operate camps, and raise funds in the area.

No matter what the style of the organization is, most large charities employ a paid staff of several hundred people. Their salaries, plus the expenses of operating the organization, come from public contributions.

The American people were rather slow to realize that a portion of their gift dollar went to maintain the charity organizations. The printed letters and brochures, the radio and television appeals were worded in such a way as to give the impression that every dime donated went directly to help crippled children or needy people, or was spent for medical research to discover a miraculous cure for a dread disease.

Because the Peter Falks and Raquel Welches and Jerry Lewises (for muscular dystrophy) and other celebrities donate their time and effort on behalf of a charity, it is only natural to assume that other, unknown people do, too. Many do. It is said that 40 million Americans do some form of volunteer charity work. Nevertheless, the management of these volunteers and the charitable organization itself is in the hands of paid workers, frequently well-paid workers.

Probably only the extremely naive and gullible believe today that every dollar they donate is spent directly to benefit recipients.* It is now widely accepted that a cer-

---

*Among the major charities, perhaps the only one that does spend all its funds for its stated purpose is the Damon Runyon-Walter Winchell

tain amount of each gift must be spent for paper and envelopes and postage, for the beautifully written and printed appeals for funds, for the advertising of children needing help in underprivileged countries, for the air time for telethons, for the circus and concert and rock performers at charity benefits. Money must also be spent to see that the money donated is properly accounted for and spent in the best ways, and it must be paid to employ talented, dedicated people to work on behalf of the charity. No one can be expected to "volunteer" full time.

The central question is not that some donations are spent to maintain the charity organization itself, but how much of the charity dollar goes for these purposes. If a person gives a dollar to a charity, how much of it is spent on raising the dollar and managing the organization? A penny? A dime, quarter, or a half dollar? Could it be as much as seventy-five or even ninety cents? In some cases it could be and is. In such instances, the public is contributing very little to the sick and needy. Most of the money is siphoned off to pay workers and those who provide services. In short, there is an awful lot of money to be made out of charity.

The major, well-known, best-run charities have become very conscious of the public's desire to know that as much of its gift dollar as possible is going for charitable purposes. They are aware that the public is measuring the effectiveness of a charity by the size of its fund-raising and management costs, and the public—thus the charities—is most conscious of fund-raising costs.

Through the years, the notion has grown that no more than 25 percent of a charity dollar should be spent on fund

Cancer Fund. Its low management and fund-raising costs are paid out of a separate fund raised for that purpose.

raising. The origin of that figure is mysterious. It may stem from the fact the United States Civil Service Commission will not allow any charity to solicit among federal employees, if it spends more than 25 percent of its income on fund raising. Wherever it comes from the idea has become widespread that a "good" charity spends less than 25 percent on fund raising while a "not so good" or "bad" charity spends more than that.

Many charity executives have pointed out that the figure is an absurdity. For a well-known charity of wide appeal, such as the United Way, the American Cancer Society, the Easter Seal Society, or CARE to spend 25 percent of its revenue on fund raising might be extremely wasteful. At the same time, a new, lesser-known charity on behalf of an unknown disease or an unpopular cause might have to spend substantially more on fund raising and still be thrifty. Exactly this point was made by Paul Funk when he explained why his Epilepsy Foundation spent a third of its money on fund raising and another 15 percent on management. His organization was new, he said, and the general public was unsympathetic to the plight of epileptics.

No one can judge what fund-raising costs ought to be. In a recent year, the Girl Scouts, generally considered a well-run charity, sold 66 million boxes of cookies at one dollar a box. From the sale the Girl Scouts made $25 million. That seems a lot, yet the Girl Scouts received only 34.7 percent of the proceeds. The remaining 62 percent was the profit made by the bakers, who submitted sealed, competitive bids, and the freight companies, who distributed the cookies. It would take a more knowledgeable person than I to state whether the Girl Scouts made a good deal. All that can be said with certainty is that the Girl Scouts executives believe they made a very good deal. The question must be asked, however, whether the same amount of money could have been raised at a lower cost in some other manner.

Another example: A favored method of raising money for charity is through a circus, concert, football game, or other athletic event. There are various arrangements, but a common one is for the circus or the athletic teams to receive a fixed amount of the receipts, say $50,000 or $100,000. This sum is paid first to the circus or teams. All receipts above that sum are then divided between the charity and the participants. Thus, if there are two athletic teams, the money above the "nut" will be split into thirds, one of which goes to the charity. If the gate is good, the charity may do well. If attendance is poor, the charity may get nothing. Is this a good way to raise money? The cost of the fund raising certainly exceeds 25 percent. Indeed, many professional fund raisers believe the principal value of a circus, an athletic event, or any other charity benefit is the promotion and good public relations it gives the charity, not the money it raises.

There are still more difficulties connected with the 25 percent figure. It is extremely hard to prove. In computing fund-raising costs, charities are supposed to include *all* the expenses of fund raising—printing, mailing, advertising, travel. These costs are also supposed to include the salaries of people involved in the fund raising. This is no particular problem for those people who work full time at fund raising. The difficulty is that they may have many duties, of which fund raising is just one.

For example, if a person opens letters, extracts checks from them, and maintains a tally of contributions, is that person's salary, as well as the cost of the business machines and data-processing equipment being used, a part of the fund-raising costs or is it a management expense under accounting? If a national officer of the charity flies to Waterloo, Iowa, meets with officials of the organization's local chapter, visits a local hospital, and speaks to the Rotary Club about the good work the charity is doing and its need to do still more, are the expenses of that trip attributable to public education, community relations, or fund raising?

Usually, the officer will attempt some fair division of his time and expenses on the trip—say, 40 percent for community service, 40 percent for public education, and 20 percent for fund raising. But the apportionment is judgmental. The fact is that the charities themselves are in the position of deciding that the time and money spent on public education and community service have been high and that the fund-raising and management costs are low. Certainly the percentages of fund-raising costs reported by even the best-run charities are something less than thoroughly reliable and comprehensive. Judging a charity by its fund-raising costs may not be a wholly reliable way to determine its effectiveness as a charity.

3

How to Start a Charity

Anyone can start a charity. All that is really needed is a cause (whether or not you believe in it), time, effort, dedication (if only to lining your pockets), and gall.

Think of a cause. Almost any will do, such as keeping America strong, protecting the environment, saving coyotes, helping unemployed youths, almost anything. Then devise an appropriate name for the charity. It will be wise to have a name that sounds high-minded and appeals to patriots or has a reference to children in it. Make it something catchy and easily remembered. You don't really need an office. It would be helpful, but you can operate the charity out of your home or car, or even out of a post-office box.

Next, draft a really socko letter. Make it as emotional as you can. Begin by scaring the reader as much as possible. Write about (depending on the cause) the danger to America from foreign or domestic menaces, the plight of the poor coyote and how the balance of nature will be damaged if it becomes extinct, or the terrible neglect of the jobless youth—whatever. Then tell what your organization is doing to correct the problem. Conclude with an appeal for support of your good work—if only a nickel or a dime.

When the letter is perfected, have it printed under your organizational letterhead in as many thousand copies as you care to mail out. The printer should also make up two envelopes. One is the outside envelope, which will contain the letter and the second envelope. The inside envelope is smaller—check size. It bears your organization's address so the contributions to your charity will arrive safely. You don't have to put postage on this return envelope, but you will probably increase your donations if you do. Simply go to the post office and sign up for a first-class mailing permit. You will pay postage only on the envelopes actually returned, and your return envelope will look very official, as though approved by the government. It will add dignity to your mailing, and at very little extra cost. After all, if you get a dollar contribution, it is little enough to pay the postage on it.

Your final step is to obtain a mailing list. This is easily done. Scores of firms are in the business of renting mailing lists at so many dollars per thousand names. There are all types of lists. You can rent one of "conservative-minded" or "liberal-minded" people, or one that is classified by age, education, geographical region, or occupation, among others.

When you have rented a list or lists, you must then address the envelopes. It would be best if you invested in automated business equipment so your letter will look official. Failing that, you could type the address on each envelope separately. You can even handwrite the address, but in that case you will sacrifice some authenticity.

Now drop all your letters in the mail and wait for the money to roll in. If your cause has appeal, and if you wrote a good solicitation letter, and if you selected a good mailing list of likely donors, quite a lot of money will roll in, perhaps millions of dollars.

As your donations arrive, you should keep a "house list" of all those people who gave you money. You will want to solicit them again next year or however often you repeat the process. As your house list grows in length, you will be able to make some money with it by renting it to other charities who want to appeal to the same type of people you do.

Can this be? Can a single individual declare himself or herself a charity and start taking in money so easily? Indeed. It has happened thousands of times for motives both noble and greedy.

Are there no regulations or laws to prevent the public from being defrauded? There are, but they are singularly weak. Perhaps the biggest threat to your newborn charity is the mail-fraud statute. You cannot use the mails to defraud people or to take money under false pretenses. If you simply pocket all the money from your "Save the Coyote Association" (or whatever), the United States postal inspectors will descend upon you sooner or later. Your only hope is to run a fly-by-night operation. Set up your charity, quickly collect all the money you can off a single mailing, then close up, move on, and start a new charity somewhere else.

You will soon be a fugitive from the law. Chances are you will be caught eventually and be prosecuted, although you may be able to operate for years and make several million dollars.

It is far better to avoid a charge of mail fraud by carrying out the purposes of your charity, however minimally. Your Save the Coyote charity might have a few brochures printed and distributed that give the history of the coyote and report its value to mankind. You might send out a few press releases to newspapers, reporting the true worth of the maligned scavenger. Even better, found a shelter for orphaned coyotes. Better still, donate a sum of money to a university or other research institution—you can even donate it to a relative, if you wish—to study the diseases of coyotes, the natural habitat of coyotes, or the reasons for public attitudes toward the predator.

You don't have to invest much money from your donations in these activities—as little as 5 or 10 percent will probably suffice—but you must do *something* on behalf of your charity to comply with mail-fraud laws. The bulk of your money, as much as 90 percent, can be spent on fund raising, paying yourself a handsome salary and expenses, paying for your office space and personal car, and hiring friends and relatives as the charity staff.

If you are truly greedy, there are several other ways to make money from your charity. You can set up a direct-mail business or an advertising or public-relations firm, then have your charity employ that company to do your fund raising for you. You might also enlist some other charities as customers and thus have two businesses going. You could buy or create mailing lists and then rent them to yourself as well as to other charities. You can find a way to rent your charity's office space from yourself or another company you own. You could engage yourself for printing and other services. You might buy "gifts" or other merchandise from yourself and send them unsolicited to prospective donors. There are myriad ways to make money. You can siphon off fifty, seventy-five, even ninety cents from each donated dollar for your own use.

Something similar has happened and does happen. Senator Mondale's subcommittee heard testimony from the Asthmatic Children's Foundation, a charity seeking to help three million boys and girls afflicted with asthma, particularly 250,000 children who suffer from a sometimes fatal form of the disease called intractable asthma.

Officers of the foundation reported that from 1963 through 1973 the foundation raised nearly $10 million, largely through direct-mail solicitation. Three quarters of this money went to V. J. Giesler & Co. of Chicago, who handled all the writing, printing, and sending of the direct-mail solicitations. Israel Friedman, the foundation's executive vice president, and other officers defended this arrangement as the most economical one available to the charity.

Of the remaining $2.5 million available to the foundation over the eleven-year period, more than $1 million went for other expenses of the foundation, including salaries, administrative costs, and payments to banks in Florida and New York, which charged a fee to open the donors' letters and to deposit the money in the foundation's accounts. Less than $1.4 million, an average of $127,000 a year, was spent on the care of asthmatic children. In other words, over the eleven-year period, an average of eighty-six cents out of every dollar collected went for fund-raising and administrative costs.

Perhaps the most pathetic part of the testimony was the evidence that the officers of the foundation were truly concerned about the plight of asthmatic children. Among those testifying was Dr. M. Murray Peshkin, a man in his eighties who had founded the organization and several hospitals for asthmatic children. He had given his whole life to the cause and had donated substantial sums of his own money to his charity, money that had mostly enriched others.

There are other regulations affecting your personal charity, but not many. A great many people labor under the misapprehension that they are protected from the charity racket by the Internal Revenue Service (IRS) of the federal government because it is empowered to issue tax exemptions to philanthropic organizations. The simple fact is that no charity need apply for a tax exemption and thousands do not. All any organization, such as your hypothetical one on behalf of coyotes, has to do is file a tax form and pay regular income taxes on the money it receives in donations. You would be foolish if you failed to do that because you would then be subject to prosecution under regular income-tax-fraud laws.

If you do apply for a tax exemption, no particular inconvenience will result. The IRS will conduct an examination to determine that your charity does indeed have a "charitable purpose." This can be almost anything, as long as your organization does not engage in a substantial amount of political campaigning or lobbying and as long as the organization is not set up in such a way as to profit the people who run it. You will be required to file an annual financial report of your organization, but even reputable charities frequently run a year or two behind in filing reports.

The IRS has the power to audit your tax-exempt report. If it finds that your organization is not carrying out its stated purposes, your exemption can be rescinded and you can be required to pay taxes on all money collected in the past. If you have openly lied on your annual reports, you can be prosecuted for giving false information under oath to the government.

All that may seem to offer the public protection against the charity racket, but it doesn't. For one thing, the IRS is undermanned and can check on only a fraction of the thousands of charities that exist. Unless the abuse is particularly flagrant, government attorneys are unlikely to prosecute. Juries feel sympathetic toward charity and dislike putting people in jail when they have had good intentions.

Even if by chance the IRS were to investigate your charity carefully, nothing in the law prevents your organization from paying fat salaries to employees or allowing them huge expense accounts. There is nothing unlawful, either, about inflated fund-raising costs, various forms of nepotism, or stupidity in spending for research, public education, and community service. Actually, the whole charity enterprise can be a joke and a waste of contributors' money and still be perfectly legal. Indeed, the IRS tax exemption may actually benefit such a charity, because it seems to lend official government approval to the racket.

Perhaps one other federal protection against wasteful and inefficient charities does exist. The Federal Trade Commission has power to stop false advertising and to prosecute those who persist in doing it. This mechanism is slow moving, however. The FTC sometimes takes years to stop a fraudulent ad campaign. In the case of charities, trouble with the FTC can probably be avoided, just as it can with the mail-fraud laws, if your organization carries out some charitable purpose, no matter how small. Thus, the advertising claims can be supported, if only a little.

There are state and local laws governing charity solicitations. If your charity wishes to solicit door to door, you may have to obtain a permit from the local government, but that usually involves no more than appearing at the appropriate office and asking for one. Such a permit offers no assurance to the contributor that the cause is genuine and that his donation will be well spent.

Some states have no laws at all regulating charity solicitations. Other states simply require a charity to register; others still want the charity to file a report of its activities. A few states impose a limitation on the organization's cost of fund raising. It is 50 percent in New York, 35 percent in Pennsylvania. A few states specify that no more than 15 percent of the money raised can be paid to a professional fund-raising solicitor. With only some exceptions, state regulation is a flimsy barrier to the charity racket, and those charities that would have difficulty complying with state laws simply avoid soliciting in the states where they are found. The officers of the Asthmatic Children's Foundation testified to the Senate subcommittee that that is what they did.

There have been some private efforts to monitor charities and to assure the public that a charity is genuine. The United Way (also known in various places by such names as the United Appeal, and the United Givers Fund) was developed to consolidate the host of charity solicitations into a single community-wide drive. A committee of the United Way, frequently called the Health and Welfare Council (HWC), decides whether a charity is suitable for participation in the drive and how much of the donations it should receive. It acts as a watchdog committee to see that participants in the United Way are legitimate charities spending money for useful purposes.

Even so, a certain amount of faith is necessary on the donor's part. The HWC considers the financial and other reports of member agencies to be confidential, not open to the public. The HWC does have the power to recommend changes in a member's administration and program, but is itself dependent for its information upon the agency's

own financial and other reports. Without doubt, however, the United Way does an effective job of policing the
activities of its member organizations. The problem is
that only a fraction of the existing charities are members of
the United Way.

Something similar happens with the State
Department's Advisory Committee on Voluntary Foreign
Aid. It monitors financial data on more than eighty charities that assist people in other countries. Unfortunately,
the information on voluntary foreign aid is confidential.

About fifteen of the larger voluntary health agencies
belong to the National Health Council, located at 1740
Broadway, New York, N.Y. 10019. This organization
regulates the health charities and applies standards to
them. For example, it has developed a system of accounting procedures for member agencies in an attempt to
make their financial reports uniform and comparable. The
council also disseminates financial and other data on the
member agencies. Unfortunately, the council represents
the member agencies as well and is largely dependent
upon the financial data they supply. It does not go behind
the reports to determine if the information is correct or
reasonable. Yet the council is a valuable source of
information on leading health charities.

The National Information Bureau is a membership
organization that attempts to provide its members with
reports on various charity organizations. Paying members of the NIB receive reports describing individual charities, providing pertinent data and sometimes describing
the organization as acceptable, not up to NIB standards,
or unacceptable. The NIB may simply report on a charity
but not evaluate it. It has a small staff and no real way to
make a reluctant charity provide it with any information,
let alone accurate information. The biggest problem with

the NIB as a public education agency is that its reports, too, are confidential and available only to NIB members.

The Council of Better Business Bureaus, with offices in 137 cities, attempts to provide information on charities. Indeed, BBB offices receive many thousands of letters and phone calls a year from people questioning a charity solicitation. Certainly the BBB is the most accessible source of information on charities and fund-raising rackets.

The council operates a Philanthropic Advisory Department in Washington headed by Helen O'Rourke, who has a staff of four. It publishes a bulletin called *Insight*, which provides brief information on charity organizations, and frequently identifies uncooperative, suspicious, or fraudulent ones.

Ms. O'Rourke's general method is to ask a charity for a report on its activities, including financial data. The data, when received, is then briefly summarized in *Insight* as a "mini-report." Organizations that fail to report are identified, and that has the effect of making it look as if they have something to hide. Ms. O'Rourke also publishes lists of organizations that have made full and partial reports to her agency. All of this information is available from local BBB offices or by mail at the Council of Better Business Bureaus, Inc., 1150 17th Street, Washington, D.C. 20036.

The problem with the BBB efforts is that Ms. O'Rourke has neither the staff nor the legal authority to go behind the reports to verify their accuracy. She is able to make no judgment on a charity's value or its work. Unfortunately, the fact that a charity did file a report with the BBB tends, whether or not that is the intent, to put a stamp of approval on the organization as a viable, publicly honest one.

Perhaps the only other way to obtain information about a charity is to write to its headquarters and ask for an annual report, but even that may prove to be a frustrating experience. Many charities are unlikely to respond at all. Others will simply send promotional literature describing the charity and its work in glowing terms. They will offer little or no financial data.

Even when financial data is provided, it is not very illuminating. The table on page 48 was provided by the National Health Council. It shows in percentages the various types of expenditures by fifteen leading health charities.

The table reveals that in a recent year the American Cancer Society, a large and well-run charity, reported that it raised $74.8 million and spent it as follows: 31.5 percent for research, 16.5 percent for public education; 10.5 percent for professional education; 7 percent for community service; 12.5 percent for patient services. This leaves 10 percent for management and general expenses and 12 percent for fund raising.

Compare this with the report of the American Lung Association, formerly known as the American Society for Tuberculosis and Respiratory Diseases. It raised $41.5 million and spent 4 percent for research; 16.5 percent for public education; 9.5 percent for professional education; 30.5 percent for community services; and 2 percent for patient services, for total program expenditures of 62.5 percent. Its managements costs were 11 percent and its fund-raising costs 24.5 percent. The remaining 2 percent was spent on acquiring property and equipment.

What is a person to conclude from a comparison of these two sets of figures? Both organizations are highly regarded charities of long duration and experience. Both are members of the National Health Council and subscribe to its uniform accounting methods. How is a person to decide which charity to give to on the basis of such financial data? Is a person to give to Cancer because it spent 31.5

Fifteen National Health Council Voluntary Health Agency Members

Program and administrative *Expenses* as Per Cent of Total Expenditures; National and Affiliate Offices
1971 or 1972

AGENCY	A Total Expenditure	B Research	C Public Education	D Professional Education	E Community Service	F Patient Service	G=B→F Total Program	H Management & General	I Fund Raising	J=H+I Total Administration	K Major Property & Equipment Acquisition
American Cancer Society	$74,852,086	31.5%	16.5%	10.5%	7%	12.5%	78%	10%	12%	22%	—
American Heart Assoc.	50,973,557	32%	12.5%	13.5%	15%	—	73%	12%	15%	27%	—
National Easter Seal Society	48,765,530	1%	2%	2%	64%	Includes Patient Ser.	69%	12%	13%	25%	6%
American Lung Assoc.	41,558,265	4%	16.5%	9.5%	30.5%	2%	62.5%	11%	24.5%	35.5%	2%
National Foundation Muscular Dystrophy Assoc.	28,799,612	15%	15%	5%	13%	19%	67%	8%	23.5%	31.5%	1.5%
Arthritis Foundation	13,619,467	24.5%	11%	3%	8%	26%	72.5%	5%	22.5%	27.5%	—
National Multiple Sclerosis Society	9,389,969	25.2%	15.5%	11%	20.5- combined		72%	14%	14%	28%	—
National Cystic Fibrosis Research Foundation	8,087,618	19.5%	12%	6%	8%	25%	70.5%	10.5%	19%	29.5%	—
Epilepsy Foundation	5,154,559	38%	19%	2%	9%	8%	76%	7%	17%	24%	—
National Hemophilia Foundation	4,082,653	4%	9%	5%	26%	8%	52%	15%	33%	48%	—
National Kidney Foundation	3,519,506	2%	3%	1.5%	2.5%	70%	79%	9%	12%	21%	—
American Diabetes Association	3,091,957	25.5%	19%	8%	11%	15%	78.5%	10%	11.5%	21.5%	—
National Soc. for the Prevention Blindness	2,603,774	9%	13%	14.5%	8%	31.5%	76%	11%	8%	19%	5%
American Social Health Assoc.	2,593,377	6.5%	34.5%	16%	20%	—	77%	8%	15%	23%	—
	634,830	27.5%	13.5%	2%	31%	—	74%	16%	10%	26%	—

National Health Council—December, 1973

percent of its money on research while Lung spent only 4 percent? Or should a person donate to Lung because it spent 30.5 percent on community services, while Cancer spent only 7 percent? Or should judgment be made on the basis of the fact that the Lung group spent more than twice as much of its money on fund raising as Cancer did? Or is it simply harder to raise money for lung diseases these days than it is for cancer?

Even when the actual figures are available, the average citizen finds it difficult to determine whether a charity is reporting accurately and fairly and spending its money wisely. The simple fact is that the American people have to accept charities on faith. There is little or no government regulation, and meaningful information is next to impossible to obtain.

Chances are that the faith of Americans in the good will and effectiveness of charity organizations is well founded, but there have been enough proven instances of abuse in the name of charity—some of them gross abuses—to add a large element of chance to this faith.

4

Professional Fund Raising

Americans are forever raising money for some purpose. They build, enlarge, or improve churches, synagogues and assorted temples, hospitals, private schools, colleges and universities, YMCAs and YWCAs, lodge halls, recreation facilities, and much, much more. They raise funds for operating budgets, endowments, and to finance scholarships and special projects. There seems to be no end to the amount of money we need for charity or the purposes for which it is spent.

Some form of fund raising is going on at any given moment. Most of the money, more than three quarters of it, is raised by religious organizations, who receive some of it in the form of cash in the offering or collection during the religious service. Many people believe the gift to be a form of worship, an offering to God. Others subscribe to a biblical injunction to tithe, that is, they give a tenth of their earnings to charity.

THE CHARITY RACKET

Most churches* today do not rely upon spontaneous or haphazard giving, but use a more businesslike approach. A church budget is prepared, frequently by a special committee with the help of the clergyman. It may include such items as payment on the church mortgage, upkeep of the building, utilities, salaries of the clergyman and others, maintenance of a church school, support of various activities, perhaps support of denominational programs.

Once the budget has been drawn up and approved by the church board and congregation, the fund raising begins. A special committee is named to supervise the fund raising. Frequently the campaign will be launched by the clergyman, who delivers an appropriate sermon during the regular services. In some churches, the lay chairperson of the fund-raising committee will explain the need for additional funds and ask members of the congregation to be more generous than they were the year before. A letter may go out to church members urging them to donate. A widespread practice is to mail each member a box of envelopes, one for each week of the year, in which to seal the check or cash. The envelopes are vital, for each member is asked to pledge so many dollars a week to the church. Pledge cards are filled out and signed at a regular church service, or members of the fund-raising committee may visit members at their homes. The sum of the members' pledges is the amount the church officers count on for operating funds during the year. When a member places the offering in the envelope each week, both the

*For simplicity, I am using the word *church* to include synagogues, temples, kingdom halls, and other such places of worship. *Congregation* refers to the worshipers collectively. Similarly, the word *clergyman* includes priests, rabbis, ministers, elders—anyone who conducts worship services.

member and the church have a record of how well the pledge is being paid. Thus, in a well-managed church, the offertory plates are piled high with envelopes. There is relatively little visible cash, most of that coming from visitors or guests, children who don't pledge, those giving more than their pledge, and a few recalcitrants who refuse to go along with the pledging process.

Thousands of other nonsectarian charitable and service organizations use similar methods to raise funds for operating budgets. Along with the pledge system go such devices as the sale of memberships, the collection of dues, and the sale of subscriptions to publications.

The time arrives at least once in the life of nearly every organization when it wants or needs to raise a substantial sum for a special purpose, such as a building fund or to increase the endowment. Relatively small sums can perhaps be raised through special appeals and special assessments on members or others in the community. But if the amount is large and difficult to raise or if the appeal must be made in a larger geographic area than usual, many organizations will then employ the services of a professional fund raiser.

As the name suggests, these are people who make their living by raising money on behalf of philanthropic organizations. A number of well-known, established fundraising firms or organizations exist. About thirty established firms belong to the American Association of Fund-Raising Counsel, Inc., which is located at 500 Fifth Avenue, New York, N.Y. 10036. The AAFRC has a full-time staff, and among its functions it acts as a clearinghouse for information about giving in the United States.

Other such organizations are the National Society of Fund Raisers, Inc., with a membership of about 1,100 in ten chapters in metropolitan areas; the American Alumni

Council; and the American College Public Relations Association. Members of the latter two groups work in the field of educational fund raising. It is estimated that as many as fifty thousand people may be employed as professional fund raisers.

To get an idea of how professional fund raisers go about their business, let us suppose that there is a project to build a new hospital in your community. The project cannot begin until people realize that a new hospital is needed. There may be none serving the community or the existing facility may be too small, old, and outmoded. If the new building is to replace an existing facility, the task is somewhat easier, for there are already experienced hospital administrators in place. But let's suppose this is an entirely new hospital.

The originators, or prime movers, of the project organize a board of trustees to operate the still nonexistent hospital. They enlist expert advice from doctors, nurses, and others familiar with hospitals, and the project begins to take shape as to a possible location for the hospital and the number of beds and various types of medical facilities it will need. An architect is brought in to design a preliminary plan for the hospital and to estimate the cost of the facility.

Suppose the fully equipped hospital—a small one—will cost about $1.5 or $1.75 million. That is a lot of money and the hospital trustees have no idea how to begin to raise it. At this point, the services of a professional fund raiser will be sought.

The fund raiser then visits the community, talks to the board of trustees, inspects plans for the project, looks over the town, and meets with important people. The purpose of these activities is to decide whether that much money can be raised in the community. He will examine local attitudes toward the hospital and toward the prime movers. What is more important, he will try to find out whether enough potential large givers live in the community. If he feels the money cannot be raised in a short time, chances are he will bow out of the project. No professional fund raiser wants to participate in a failure if he can help it.

Let's assume that in this case, he decides the money can be raised for the hospital and agrees to go ahead. The hospital trustees will try to raise $2 million, of which $200,000 is the cost of raising the funds.

It is axiomatic that the fund raiser never personally asks anyone for a nickel. All solicitation is done by local citizens. In fact, the fund raiser will be invisible to all but the trustees and other leaders of the campaign.

An early task is to select a fund-raising committee. The fund raiser and the trustees will select an individual as campaign chairperson who is well known and respected in the community, such as a doctor, banker, clergyman, or business executive. Other members of the campaign committee will be scarcely less important. It is bound to include a banker to solicit from bankers, a corporate executive to call upon other executives, a small businessperson to ask for donations from stores, a labor leader to call upon unions and workers, a farmer to solicit from farmers. The whole community will be organized not only into types of business or profession, but geographically for house-to-house solicitation. The town will be broken down into sections and blocks with a person in charge of solicitations in each. No likely or even unlikely source of contributions will be ignored.

The fund raiser knows, however, that most of the money will come from a few people. A rule of thumb is that 80 percent of the money must come from 20 percent of the people. Therefore, the first act of the fund raiser is to identify in his own mind who the large contributors are likely to be. This list is refined in conversations between the fund raiser and the campaign committee. In short, the potential large donors are rated in terms of how much money they can be expected to give. The rating takes into consideration such factors as the known or guessed wealth of the donor, the donor's reputation for generosity, or his or her attitude toward the hospital project.

Out of these discussions comes a "giving chart." In the case of our hypothetical hospital, it might identify two individuals who would give $100,000 each, five who would give $50,000 each, thirty who are likely to give $25,000 each, fifty who might donate $5,000 each, and a hundred $1,000 givers. This adds up to $1,500,000, with the rest of the money coming from smaller gifts from the general public.

Before the campaign officially opens, a select group, made up perhaps of the campaign chairman and a couple of the hospital trustees, will visit the principal potential donors. They will inform each of these people of the great need for the hospital and hint in various ways—mostly suggested by the professional fund raiser—that they expect a check for a certain amount. It is not easy to ask a person to give a large amount, like $100,000, but the professional fund raiser is experienced at it. Wealthy individuals will part with such sums if they believe the cause is worthy, if it has tax advantages for them, and if they derive from it feelings of generosity, power, and public spiritedness.

The professional's job is to find the right message that will untie the purse strings of large donors. Customarily, 30 to 40 percent of the funds will be raised or pledged in this manner prior to the official opening of the campaign.

This gives a tremendous boost to the efforts of all the other campaign workers, and the giving public will feel a desire to jump on the bandwagon and put the campaign over the top with a few extra dollars.

Working behind the scenes, the fund raiser develops a theme and slogan for the campaign. He arranges to have the support of the newspapers and radio and television stations. He and his staff prepare press releases and radio and TV spots and encourage feature stories and programs in the media. They will dispatch speakers to address various clubs and organizations, and recommend clever gimmicks and novel, exciting fund-raising approaches, such as a children's pet show or a beauty contest. The purpose of it all is to make the hospital, the campaign, and the campaign committee as visible as possible and to keep the campaign workers enthusiastic. Perhaps the most difficult task of the fund raiser is to maintain the morale of the volunteers and keep them working. He is a stern taskmaster, a shoulder to cry on, and a source of expert advice—sometimes all three at the same time.

It should all be over in a short time. Luckily the hospital trustees have raised their money, the fund raiser has earned his fee, and everyone is happy.

Obviously, the opportunities for the professional fund raiser to make a little money for himself on the side are considerable. Even if he doesn't actually steal donations by failing to report them, juggle the books, or make deals with other fund raisers or contributors, he is still in a position to extract secret kickbacks from printers, photographers, artists, caterers, and other businessmen. At a minimum, he could run up expenses unnecessarily and claim an extra fee for unexpected costs. There is a history of all this.

The American Association of Fund-Raising Counsel

tries to eliminate this by developing and publicizing a code of ethics for fund raisers. First, fund raisers are to serve only nonprofit agencies with a known, reputable purpose. Second, fund raisers never get a percentage of the money raised; they receive a flat fee that is agreed upon in advance and never changed. Also, no fund raiser is to accept a commission or kickback from suppliers. Third, the fund raiser in charge must have six years of experience in the profession. Fourth, no exaggerated claims of past success or guaranteed results should be used in soliciting clients. Fifth, no fund raiser should make a payment to a charity or one of its officers to gain employment as a fund raiser.

The AAFRC recommends that when charities choose a fund raiser they should deal with reputable fund-raising counsels, talk to former clients of the counsel about their experiences with the firm, and discuss all matters with the potential fund raiser until they reach a full understanding of methods to be used and the fee to be charged.

The question of payment for a professional fund raiser is a controversial one. Some fund raisers believe that a fee that is a percentage of the money raised or the goal of money to be raised is best. It ensures that the fund raiser will work hard and be imaginative in his efforts. However, the AAFRC forbids this for its members, as do some state laws, and recommends a flat fee instead. The AAFRC maintains that a percentage fee may result in too large a payment to the fund raiser. He may be paid a commission on oral or unconfirmed pledges that are never paid to the charity. Also, many donors resent giving a percentage of their gifts to a professional. They may downgrade their donation accordingly or wait until the fund raiser has left town to make their gift. The flat fee helps the charity to avoid these problems, guarantees that the fund raiser will work a specified number of hours, and includes payment for employees, printing, and other expenses.

So how much do professionals charge? No one says exactly, but the AAFRC publishes these figures: Twenty-two capital campaigns for higher education raised over $124 million at a median cost of 5 percent. Another twenty-seven capital campaigns for secondary schools raised nearly $27 million at a median cost of 5.1 percent. Still another eighty-six capital campaigns for hospitals raised $173 million at a median cost of 4.75 percent. These figures included budgeted expenses as well as the fixed fee.

The fee varies with the amount of money to be raised, the difficulty there will be in raising it, and the type of campaign to be used. The expenses of a mail campaign, for example, would be greater than those for a direct solicitation. Professional fund raisers reported in private conversation that fund-raising costs of 10 percent are normal, less than that a virtue.

Large universities and certain other types of nonprofit institutions employ a full-time, in-house fund raiser. He and his staff work year round to garner money for institution's operating budget, endowment, and special projects. This type of fund raiser will be far more visible than the one-shot professional just described. He will usually have a title and represent the institution on fund-raising occasions.

He will seek funds from a variety of sources such as government grants and contracts, grants from foundations, bequests from individuals, and corporate gifts. Each type of solicitation must be carefully attuned to the needs and desires of the donor. Where a dowager might give money to have a building named after her, a corporation might want to support a specific type of research program.

In colleges and universities, as well as private schools, the alumni are an important source of contributions. No effort is disregarded by the fund raiser to raise money, and alumni giving starts when a person is a student, at least in the sense that the school inculcates a pride and gratitude toward the alma mater that will follow the graduates through all the years of alumni giving. After graduation the alumni will receive regular brochures and other news of the colleges, and, particularly if they turn out to be well-to-do and generous, they may be honored with alumni awards and membership in various special societies of distinguished alumni. In some cases, the school will confer an honorary degree upon them.

Mostly, however, the alumni are barraged with solicitation letters appealing to their generosity. The letters are generally written by the college fund raiser or his staff and mailed out over the signature of a well-known member of each graduating class, who acts as "class agent."

Universities and philanthropic institutions also raise funds by electing quite a large board of trustees, composed for the most part of wealthy bankers, corporate executives, and professional people. Expertise in educational matters is usually not required or even desirable among trustees, but a fat purse is frequently a prerequisite.

Whatever else a fund raiser may be, he is expected to have "contacts." He is supposed to know his way around government offices, corporate headquarters, foundation board rooms, and the homes of the wealthy. He is expected to know where the charity dollar is and how to get it.

PROFESSIONAL FUND RAISING

What is to be made of all this? It would seem that given our system of private colleges and universities, private hospitals, and private religious and other eleemosynary institutions, the reputable professional fund raiser performs a vital function. If his fee and expenses come to only 10 or even 15 percent of the money raised, then he is far more efficient than most of the well-known and much-supported charities in the nation.

Unfortunately, not all professional fund raisers are reputable. Charity in America has produced over the years some first-class scoundrels and thieves. It is not just that the sums of money involved were large, but that the money was given to some of our most highly regarded charities by a defenseless public. Somehow robbing disabled veterans and polio victims seems more heinous than robbing a bank.

A number of ways can be found to rob even the best-intentioned charity. A reputable fund raiser never interferes in the management of a charitable organization. He merely counsels the organization on how best to raise funds. A disreputable fund raiser not only interferes with the management, he also recommends how the money ought to be spent and tries, if possible, to gain control of the charity's funds. Some examples of this are reported in the next chapter.

A reputable fund raiser does not solicit funds on his own behalf. His entire payment is the fee or commission negotiated in his contract. A disreputable fund raiser siphons off funds in various ways. One, as we have seen, is to engage in costly fund-raising methods that divert 85 or 90 percent of the donations into the hands of the fund raiser.

Another method is to take a moribund charity or non-profit association that has tax-exempt status and to use it as a front for a phony charity created by the fund raiser. The phony charity launches a quick, blitz mail campaign. The money received is consumed in expenses—perhaps incurred with the fund raiser's own direct-mail firm—and paid to the fund raiser and his associates in salaries and consulting fees.

Perhaps the most infamous fund raiser, who serves as an example of many of these techniques as well as a few others, was Abraham Koolish. Koolish entered the big-money charity racket in 1943 with the Disabled American Veterans. He struck charity gold with something known as the ident-o-tag, which was a miniature replica of an individual motorist's car-license tag. As refined, the tiny tag was encased in plastic and equipped with a chain so that car keys could be attached to it. The tag was offered to a beguiled wartime public—a public that would do anything on behalf of disabled veterans—as a public service. Should the car keys be lost, the finder would return them to the DAV, who would then see that they were returned to the owner.

The tag seemed useful, although it did occur to some people that the ident-o-tag offered a means by which the finder of lost keys could identify the vehicle to which the keys belonged and then use the keys to steal it. Nonetheless, the tags were popular. Lots of people, receiving the device in the mail, sent in a donation to the DAV. Lots and lots of people. Koolish mailed out more than eight million of the tags in 1943 alone. He charged DAV $62.50 per thousand for the tags and for the letter that was sent with it. In that year, out of a total of $800,000 raised, Koolish received about $500,000 from the DAV for his efforts, leaving about $300,000 for the veterans' organization.

In 1945, the DAV decided to go into the ident-o-tag business for itself and generously paid Koolish $1.3 million for his device, even though it was not patented and could have been used by anyone. Koolish was also paid a thousand dollars a month as a consultant.

Koolish soon set up another organization, the National Association of Veterans Employment Councils. With millions of World War II veterans mustering out of the service and looking for work, it was a splendid idea. Koolish raised almost $2 million in two years, spent practically all of it on fund raising, and then folded.

His next ingenious idea, designed to capitalize on the postwar baby boom, was National Kids Day. It enlisted the support of several celebrities and a number of reputable community organizations. National Kids Day caught on. After all, everyone loves kids. Koolish raised over $4 million in five years and spent 92 percent of it on fund raising and public relations. Most of the money was paid to Gayton Associates, a fund-raising firm owned by Koolish. A number of celebrities, including Bing Crosby, complained that their names were being used without permission, and the day for the kids became defunct.

All of this was just a warm-up for Koolish's next charitable enterprise. In 1949, he entered into a fund-raising contract with the Sister Kenny Institute, a most respected organization in Minneapolis that treated polio patients. With his genius for fund raising, Koolish raised $22 million for the Institute between 1951 and 1960. Of this amount, only $9 million went to the Institute to help polio victims. The remainder was divided between Koolish and Marvin Kline, former mayor of Minneapolis, who had become the institute's executive director. In effect, Koolish and Kline pocketed the $13 million and hid the expropriation under phony fund-raising and public-education costs.

The two men might have gotten away with it had they

quit a little earlier—the Salk vaccine had already made polio an ex-charity—or been a little less greedy, but their thievery was so bald-faced that it commanded the attention of a young man serving as Minnesota's attorney general. He investigated, uncovered the fraud, and saw Koolish and Kline each sentenced to ten years in prison for mail fraud. The attorney general is now Senator Walter F. Mondale, whose interest in charity fraud led to the hearings by the Senate Subcommittee.

It would be pleasant to believe that Koolish's activities and methods of milking charities are unique or even rare. They may well be. The hard fact is that no one really knows—and there is no orderly process for finding out.

5

In the Name of Religion

> Congress shall make no law respecting an establishment of religion, or prohibiting the free exercise thereof. . . .

Those words, the first in the Bill of Rights, the hallowed document of American freedom, have helped to make the United States a citadel of religious freedom and tolerance. To be sure, our history is studded with episodes of religious prejudice and even violence. Yet the United States has hosted a wide, even bewildering variety of religions. In recent decades, all have come to exist side by side amicably.

The First Amendment has also helped to make the United States perhaps unique in the world as a haven for crackpot religions, religious cults, and out-and-out religious swindles. We have produced or embraced from abroad hundreds of religious "leaders," "holy" men and women, soothsayers, visionaries, high priests and priestesses, yogis, gurus, reincarnations of Christ, con men, and swindlers, each one seemingly more colorful and bizarre than the last. Americans have donated untold sums, surely hundreds of millions of dollars, to these religions. This goes on today unabated.

The problem is to distinguish between a genuine or authentic religion and a self-serving swindle. The Bible says that God works in mysterious ways. Yesterday's oddball religion is today's respected denomination. Every major religion and sect was denounced at its inception as heretic and its adherents were persecuted. In Western culture, the Jews were persecuted by the Egyptians and the Romans. The Christians were persecuted by the pagans and the Romans. The Christians, in turn, persecuted the Jews and launched the crusades against the Muslims. Christianity split first into Roman Catholic and Eastern Orthodox. Then the Protestants split from the Catholics. The Protestants then divided into hundreds of sects. The United States has given rise to several sects that survived derision and persecution to become established and respected, notably the Mormons, the Seventh Day Adventists, the Christian Scientists, and the Jehovah's Witnesses.

Again, yesterday's cult has a way of becoming today's respected religious denomination. Therefore it can be foolhardy to denounce a religious practice, however bizarre, as a fraud being perpetrated on the public. Law-enforcement officers dislike such investigations. Prosecutors shy away from them in court. Congressional committees and other regulatory agencies give them a wide berth. The Better Business Bureau in its reports on charity rackets refuses to make any comment on religious practices.

All of this has left the door wide open for some truly

exotic and rascally swindles in the name of religion. In fact, there have been so many cults and rip-offs that it is hard to select a few of the juiciest.*

Perhaps the most famous preacher of modern times was Aimee Semple McPherson. As "Sister Aimee," she preached before millions of Americans and was heard by millions more on the radio. She was possibly the most dynamic, flamboyant, and effective evangelical preacher ever to appear on these shores.

Aimee was a rather tragic figure. Born in Ontario, Canada, in 1890, she was converted by a wandering Pentecostal preacher named Robert Semple, whom she married. Semple took her to China as a missionary, and then died. After the birth of her daughter, Aimee struggled to get back home as far as New York. She underwent a period of hardship and near starvation and then married a staid grocery clerk named Harold S. McPherson, by whom she had a son. But the marriage did not last, because Aimee had an irresistible urge to preach as Semple had. All her life she seemed torn between the desire to live a normal life as a housewife and mother and the need to hold center stage as a preacher moving crowds to her will.

Aimee returned to Canada and began gaining experience as a preacher. Her theology was rather straightforward Pentecostal. As Richard Mathison points out, she did not form a religious cult, although she behaved like a cult leader. The Pentecostal beliefs embraced by Aimee were baptism by fire and speaking in tongues, divine healing through prayer, the imminent second coming of

*One of the best, most readable accounts of this subject is *Faiths, Cults and Sects of America* by Richard Mathison (Bobbs-Merrill Co., Indianapolis and New York, 1960). A soft-cover edition was published in 1962 under the title *God Is a Millionaire.*

Christ, and spiritual and physical redemption through Christ's crucifixion and scourging.

Somehow Aimee was able to take this fairly common-place theology and turn it into a cult. From her arrival in Los Angeles in 1918 until her death in 1944, she was front-page news, the biggest religious celebrity in America. No auditorium was big enough for her. She spoke to overflow crowds of fifteen to twenty thousand people several times a day, not just in Los Angeles but all over the country.

She mixed old-time religion and show biz to create spectacles never seen before or since. At the height of her fame, she used to stand on the stage, attired in a white, flowing gown, clutching a bouquet of roses, which she threw one by one to the adoring thousands before her. She was accompanied by a brass band and a choir of four hundred beautiful girls. She regularly led the band and choir, and her adoring followers, on street parades.

As the dollars flowed in by the millions, she built a temple in Los Angeles where she began to stage the equivalent of vaudeville shows. Since Pentecostalists were forbidden to go to the theater, she took the theater to them, staging elaborate and expensive "illustrated sermons" in which biblical tales were acted out in pantomime while she read the text and interpreted it. She imported costumes from all over the world, and hired theatrical equipment and technicians to operate it. Her shows were unique and splendid. The money rolled in.

By the mid-1920's, Aimee Semple McPherson changed in the public's eye from being a respected evangelist to a sort of side-show freak. She became a glamour girl, who was always lavishly attired in Paris gowns. She lived in luxurious houses and drove expensive cars. Having once been poor, she made up for it by thrusting her wealth forward as proof of her success. Her romantic escapades made headlines, as did the tales of sexual orgies inside her temple. Her mother and daughter left her and denounced her, then sued her in court. She became involved in legal actions over a highly suspicious tale she told about being kidnapped. She was offered contracts to star in movies and planned to do a movie of her own life.

No scandal, no court action, no denouncement of her from other pulpits could diminish the loyalty of her followers. She died in 1944, from an overdose of sleeping pills, and her funeral was an orgy of emotion in which her faithful wept, swooned, and begged God to send her back.

Aimee's temple passed to the control of her son, who lacked her oratorical and theatrical skills. The church gradually became a rather ordinary and respected Pentecostal temple.

Joe Jeffers was hardly as celebrated as Aimee Semple McPherson, but he parlayed a mellifluous voice and seemingly boundless gall into a career as a religious con man that spanned four decades. In so doing, he survived enough legal and criminal problems to have ended the careers of a dozen men.

In the 1920's, he was a highly regarded fundamentalist preacher of the hellfire and brimstone type in the Southwest. In the 1930s, he surfaced in Los Angeles preaching a form of gospel that reeked of anti-Semitism. He had seized upon the discredited theology that the British people were the "Lost Tribe of Israel." His sermons blamed the Jews for the world's problems and were thus highly similar to the rantings of Adolf Hitler, whose Nazi party had come to power in Germany.

The racist stench of Jeffers' preaching led to efforts to discredit him. In 1939, he and his wife Joy were brought into court on a morals charge. The trial was the most lurid and the most sexually explicit in the history of Los Angeles, and huge crowds filled the courthouse hoping to see the secret movie made of the Jeffers' activities. The couple was acquitted, not because the charges weren't true, but because Joy and Joe were legally married and the jury considered the film an invasion of their privacy.

The publicity would have ruined another man, but Jeffers survived, bigger than ever.

His next legal problem came when Joy divorced him. He fled to Florida in her car and spent fifteen months in a Florida prison for interstate transportation of a stolen car.

Being an ex-con did not stop Jeffers. In the late 1940's, he reappeared in Los Angeles where he had somehow acquired the money to buy a million-dollar mansion on five acres in Laurel Canyon. Here, claiming to be the messenger of God, who lived in the constellation Orion, he founded the "Kingdom of Yahweh." He induced numbers of people to turn over all their worldly possessions to the Kingdom and take up residence there. Soon Jeffers had a gorgeous green-eyed, blond second wife, Irene, who was declared his "high priestess."

Equally soon, Jeffers was in trouble with the law again. Laurel Canyon neighbors complained of noise and bacchanalian orgies inside the Kingdom. Disgruntled members of the Kingdom sued to recover their property. First wife Joy kept suing for back alimony. The law moved in and returned Jeffers to prison as a parole violator.

By the time Jeffers was released from prison in the 1950's, the Kingdom of Yahweh had folded in Los Angeles and had reopened in Denver under the ministrations of Irene. As the "green virgin," she stood before the crowds adorned in a diaphanous gown and preached the joys of love. Jeffers joined in, claiming to be in touch with Jesus, who still lived in India, and with Yahweh in Orion. Joe and Irene had some good years but finally fell out and were divorced. Jeffers moved on to Phoenix, Arizona, but hurried back when Irene was found brutally murdered in her temple. He proclaimed that she had gone to Orion to sit on the right hand of Yahweh, and that she now related to him the secrets of the universe.

Jeffers returned to Phoenix with a third beautiful wife, Connie, who had been Irene's secretary. He began to preach reincarnation and claimed, for a fee, that he could provide a portrait of a person as he or she had looked in a previous life. He wrote to his followers around the country and received money for his reincarnation portraits. United States postal inspectors gradually built a case against Jeffers. A woman was found in West Virginia who had been hired to paint portraits for him. She thought it strange that she had been instructed not to let the portraits resemble any known person. When evidence was found that Joe and Connie were spending the money from the reincarnation portraits at the local racetracks, Jeffers was convicted and jailed for mail fraud.

A religion dubbed the "Mighty I am" would seem to be automatically suspect, yet Guy Ballard, a salesman, and his wife Edna, a professional medium, developed it into a cult that claimed hundreds of thousands of followers and earned the couple an estimated $3 million. Ballard claimed that on a visit to Mount Shasta he had been visited by the legendary Count St. Germain, an eighteenth-century nobleman reported to be immortal. St. Germain had fed Ballard a potion, he said, and had then taken him on a trip through time to see the mysteries of the universe unveiled.

In his writing and in his preaching, during which he

wore a white suit with a pink tie, Ballard claimed to be the reincarnation of various historic figures and to have secret powers, including the ability to make himself invisible. He could guarantee immortality. Hadn't Jesus personally returned for twenty-one days to pose for the painting that was on sale in the lobby of his temple? Ballard also claimed to have seen a great underground lake of gold. For a suitable donation, he could arrange for the faithful to obtain a bucketful.

After Ballard's death in 1940, Edna tried to carry on his work, but she, her son, and twenty-two others were convicted of mail fraud, although the Supreme Court later overturned the conviction on a technicality.

The list of bizarre religions is a long one. There was a Ben Purnell, who announced that he was the Seventh Messenger sent by God to save the world. He, like so many other cultists, organized a community. His was called the House of David. For years there were House of David baseball and basketball teams, the players all wearing full beards. Purnell repeatedly fled to Canada to escape morals and fraud charges. He was eventually caught, having hidden out for years in an underground room. His weight was down to a hundred pounds, but that didn't seem to bother the bevy of ladies in nightwear who lived with him. He was tried and convicted, but died soon after that.

Franz Creffield, who billed himself as "Joshua the Second," caused a sensation in the small town of Corvallis, Oregon. A principal tenet of his religion, which he called the Church of the Bride of the New Prophet, was that the parishioners, mostly female, had to disrobe during the service and the private conversations with the pastor. This ritual increased his following, but caused some anger among the male citizens of the area. Eventually, Creffield was murdered by a young man who contended his sister had been led into an immoral life by Joshua. The parishioners were distraught. Such was the loyalty to Creffield that the wronged girl embraced her brother and, as she did so, shot him in the head.

There was the ghastly Aleister Crowley, who traveled much of the world, including the United States, titillating the jaded rich with bestial, orgiastic versions of the Satanic black mass. Edvaard Admusson and an attractive high priestess founded a cult in Baja California to worship the ancient Egyptian god Isis, then absconded with funds donated by the gullible. There was also a succession of Hindu gurus, yogis, and maharajahs, real and fake, such as Khrishna Venta and his barefoot people, and Khrish-namurti, who was the "mouth-piece of God." Finally there was John Briggs, who started a community in Arizona. All went well with the Briggs group until the houses were built and the time came for the "sacred marriages." All the women were lined up on one side and the men on the other. As the Leader, Briggs, adorned in a black velvet cape with the number 9 emblazoned on it, selected his nine wives first. Briggs's nine councilors, known as De-vouts, each took nine wives too. The ten women left un-selected were declared "princesses' and were to pick nine husbands apiece. Briggs declared everyone married, and they all adjourned to their respective houses.

Problems and jealousies inevitably arose. Many of the wives of the Devout felt neglected, while the princesses devoutly wished they might be. Finally, a disgruntled Devout headed for the authorities 175 miles away. When this treachery was discovered, the members of the com-mune fled, and none of them was seen again.

The formation of cults and new religions is anything

but ancient history in the United States. Since the mid-1960's, thousands of communes and similar organizations have been established in this country. Some are religiously oriented, such as the Children of God, the extended family, Ontology, Hare Krishna, and Zen Buddhism. Some are back-to-nature movements, with their members seeking a simpler, more natural existence. A few are thinly veiled excuses for bizarre sexual conduct and the use of narcotics. And, alas, there are others that are organized for violent purposes.* In some cases, the violence is politically motivated, as with the Weathermen, the Minutemen, and the Symbionese Liberation Army. There are also cases of violence for violence's sake, notably the commune that followed Charles Manson into eight brutal murders in California. Long after Manson was imprisoned, one of his female followers attempted to shoot President Ford.

In his book *Faiths, Cults and Sects of America*, Richard Mathison sought to portray the type of person who joins a religious cult. In general, he wrote, the cultist is poor, confused, uprooted from family ties, disenchanted with the more conventional religion learned as a child, disappointed with his or her ambitions, and disaffected from society as a whole. The more demanding the faith and the more bizarre the cult, the more it appeals to such people, because it tests their emotions and not their reason and gives them the feeling of being a special person, chosen by God. Mathison added:

*This is a book about charities and not about fraud *per se*. A person does not usually think of it in terms of charity, but mention should be made of the billions of dollars that the American people have contributed over the years to political campaigns. At least a portion of it has gone to demagogues and scoundrels who acted in their own self-interest, abused the American political system, and sometimes sought to destroy it.

IN THE NAME OF RELIGION

A cult leader knows that the more incredible the beliefs he can promulgate, the more assured he is of building a solid core of devotees who will defend themselves against the outside world of cynics and actually become more malleable because of their persecution.

The American people have long had a special difficulty in defending themselves against charlatans who line their pockets in the name of religion. This is due to our history of religious toleration and the guarantees of the First Amendment. In banning school prayers in 1962, the Supreme Court reiterated the concept that religion is an entirely private affair in America. Our Constitution and our laws defend the right of every person to worship any God in any way he wishes, or none at all—and even to make a fool of himself in doing so. Thus it was not at all strange that when the defector left John Briggs's commune in Arizona and told authorities of the bizarre goings-on there, he was laughed at.

Perhaps our only protection against religious charlatans is the mail-fraud statute. It can work only if the mails are used to solicit money, and then under the greatest difficulty, because it must be proved that the money solicited was used for personal enrichment and not for some religious purpose. The extreme difficulty of such proof makes the United States a particular haven for religious fraud.

It must be pointed out that the cultists themselves are not the only victims. Some of our most conservative and best-run religious organizations have been taken in. A well-known case occurred in the 1950's, when a "wealthy" Washington attorney named Victor Orsinger victimized the Society of the Divine Savior, a Catholic religious order and charity. Orsinger offered a facade of personal wealth and business acumen at a time when his various enterprises were short of cash. He talked the leaders of the Society into allowing him the opportunity to apply his business skills to the charity's capital fund, thereby greatly increasing its value.

As proof of his noble intentions, Orsinger gave large sums to the Society and to other Catholic organizations. Orsinger used the Society as a front for various shady business dealings, and meanwhile began to siphon off several hundred thousand dollars from the various groups. He also embezzled a million dollars from the Sisters of the Divine Saviour in Milwaukee.

Other businessmen were suspicious of Orsinger's activities, but were intimidated into silence because he represented a well-known religious order. Eventually, his charity-fronted empire collapsed—and took several religious orders into bankruptcy with him.

In the 1960's, a Texas promoter, Frank Sharp, victimized the Jesuit Fathers of Houston and drove them into bankruptcy too. Sharp won the confidence of the Jesuits by giving them a large tract of land and by making Father Michael Kennelly a director of his bank. Father Kennelly was pleased to be the first priest ever named a bank director in America, and to show his appreciation he gave Sharp $6 million in charity funds to invest—money that was never repaid.

The priest showed his appreciation in other ways. He acted as intermediary, whether or not he knew that was what he was doing, in Sharp's bribery of several Texas politicians. Father Kennelly also arranged for Sharp to become the first Protestant honored by the Father General of the Jesuit Order, and made it possible for him and his family to have a private audience with Pope Paul VI in Rome. Ultimately, Sharp was exposed by the Securities and Exchange Commission, the federal regulatory agency that watchdogs stock frauds. He served a jail sentence for larceny.

More recently, in 1974, the Pallottines, a Roman Catholic order in Baltimore, spent more than $1.9 million to mail out 106 million computerized fund-raising letters. *The Baltimore Sun* estimated that the mailing, which included a sweepstakes contest, raised up to $15 million. Yet the order's accounts show that out of this money it received less than half a million dollars in cash and supplies.

The Pallottines have been mentioned in connection with the indictment of Maryland's governor and five others, because they admitted lending their real-estate advisor, Dennis Webster, $54,000. Mr. Webster, who was treasurer for Governor Mandel's reelection campaign, is reported to have lent that same amount of money to the governor. In addition, the Pallottines invested $280,000 in a company of which Mr. Webster was president.

The evidence seems unmistakable that even though a charity calls itself a religion or is operated by a religious group or in the name of a religion, scant protection is possible against fraud. Religion may, in fact, invite it. Perhaps more heed should be given to two rather cynical statements. Clarence Darrow, the famous lawyer, wrote in his *Autobiography*: "Nothing is so eagerly believed as that which is not so." Even more to the point is a statement by the writer-editor H. L. Mencken: "The surest way to get-rich-quick in this country, next to robbing a bank, is to start a new religion."

6

Anything for Kids

A sure-fire way for a charity to appeal to American generosity is through children. Basil O'Connor and the National Foundation showed the way by calling polio "infantile paralysis" and depicting children rather than adult victims. If it is at all possible, most charities will use children to raise funds. Foreign-aid charities regularly urge that Americans adopt a child overseas. Such appeals strike at a basic human desire to protect children from pain and want.

Fund raising is even more effective when children solicit donations. For many years, UNICEF has had children pass the collection box along with the trick-or-treat bag on Halloween. The Girl Scouts have made their annual cookie sales a national institution. The Campfire Girls also sell door to door, mostly candy and nuts, but calendars and magazine subscriptions as well. Many other youth groups sell such items as candy, Christmas cards, greeting cards, and candles.

These sales are normally well supervised. The Girl Scouts are allowed to sell only in their immediate neighborhoods or among family members and friends. When selling, they must go in pairs, observe traffic laws, and wear their uniforms so they are identifiable.

Most of the merchandise sold by young people is purchased from reputable companies and is of good quality. The financial arrangements are made in advance. When the public buys something from an organization like the Scouts or the Campfire Girls, it realizes that while it may be paying a somewhat higher price for it, the product is good and the price includes a donation to the charity. These organizations defend their fund-raising techniques by saying that they give the children a chance to meet the public and to learn salesmanship, record keeping, and the handling of money. Such charity sales by children are first cousins to the practice of hiring boys and girls as newspaper carriers.

Just the same, house-to-house sales by children became so lucrative a charity fund raiser that operators inevitably began to transform it into a racket. Senator Mondale's Subcommittee on Children and Youth turned up several such cases.

The most bald-faced operated in several Midwestern states. Morrie Friedman, described as the executive director of the National Youth Clubs of America, told how his organization operated. The principal purpose of the clubs was to sell, from house to house, candy manufactured by the E. G. Whitman Company of Bridgeport, Pennsylvania. Friedman said that in 1973 the National Youth Clubs had a gross revenue of about $1 million. About half the money came from the sale of candy; the other half came from the sale of franchises to sell candy.

The way the scheme worked, individuals (whom Mr.

Friedman referred to as "wealthy") would put up about $5,000 for a National Youth Clubs franchise—that is, the right to sell the organization's candy in a certain territory. In addition to the license to sell, the franchise owner was let in on certain "trade secrets," as Mr. Friedman called them. These were the techniques for selling candy door to door.

The techniques were not complicated. The franchise owner hired "crew managers," who recruited children between the ages of roughly eight and fourteen to act as salespersons. After school or perhaps on a Saturday, the crew manager drove the children several miles from their homes, and left them on a street corner with a supply of E. G. Whitman candies. The children were told to knock on doors and tell people they were from the National Youth Clubs and that they were trying to earn money for scholarships. After several hours, the children were picked up at a prearranged location and returned to their homes by the crew managers.

The children were paid twenty-five cents for each box of candy they sold. The remaining $1.25 or $1.50 of the sales price was divided among the crew manager, the franchise owner, the National Youth Clubs, and the E. G. Whitman Company. What of the scholarships? Mr. Friedman said the National Youth Clubs recommended that the distributors set aside two percent of their receipts as a scholarship fund, but he admitted that his organization had no power to enforce compliance. He said he thought a few $25 savings bonds had been given to the children who had sold the most candy.

Mr. Friedman testified that twenty-five to thirty thousand children were employed as salespersons by his organization.

Senator Mondale asked him a pertinent question:

"What do you call your enterprise? National Youth Clubs? Would not this name lead the public to believe that you were running a charitable enterprise rather than a business?"

Friedman replied, "Probably."

A second, similar organization spotlighted by the subcommittee was Youth Incentives, Inc., whose founder, Gerald Winters, testified. He described himself as a candy manufacturer and distributor based in Florida. He was concerned about the plight of young blacks in the ghetto, and he realized that the difference between them and the more affluent white youths in the suburbs was the amount of money jangling in their pockets. If young people in the ghetto were given a chance to earn money, they would learn the value of honest work, discover how to handle money, and stop hanging around street corners getting into trouble. Even better, by selling candy house to house in the suburbs, they would get out of the ghetto and find out how other people lived, and their aspirations would be raised accordingly.

Mr. Winters and other men formed Youth Incentives groups in New York, New Jersey, Florida, and other states. Ghetto youths—Mr. Winters vehemently insisted that a thirteen-year-old from the ghetto was a youth and not a child—were recruited, driven to various locations, sometimes on quite long trips, and set to selling candy door to door. At least some of the candy was manufactured by Mr. Winters. He said he had made about $1 million from the enterprise. The youths were paid about twenty-five cents a box and were given their money at the end of each work day. Mr. Winters felt it was an advantage to have them receive the money earned by their efforts immediately.

Both Mr. Friedman and Mr. Winters admitted they had encountered some legal difficulties. They had been arrested for violations of various local peddling and licensing laws, as well as state and federal child-labor laws. Both men felt somewhat persecuted by the law. Mr. Friedman felt that children who sold candy from door to door were not much different from those who delivered newspapers. Mr. Winters felt he was being harassed because he was trying to help black youths.

The Senate Subcommittee also called upon several state charity licensing officials to testify concerning the youthful candy-selling enterprises. Donald G. Mulack of the Illinois Charitable Contributions Division identified several similar organizations that operated in his state, such as United Youths of America, United Boys Group, United Youth Group, Opportunity for Youth, Employment for Youth, and Student Opportunities for Achievement. He described the operations in this way:

> Our investigation has found that although the descriptive name suggests the organization is benefitting youth, none of the above organizations have established any youth clubs in the ordinary understanding of that term. On the contrary, the organizations were created to make fast money for the promoters, with only incidental benefits to the children employed.
>
> Further, most of these organizations are void of permanency, and instead operate out of storefronts with constantly changing locations as regulatory agencies continually expose their procedures. In several such operations the headquarters were located in the trunk of an auto or motel room that could disappear overnight.
>
> In a typical operation, a crew manager recruits young people at candy stores near grammar schools through posters and flyers which advertise:—"Students Wanted, earn up to $20 a Week, part-time." Only a telephone number is listed. When a

student calls, arrangements are made for his indoctrination and transportation with other children, in crews of five, to affluent neighborhoods in the suburbs.

A typical representation by the child is that they are working for scholarships, prizes or vacations. Our investigation of the National Youth Clubs of America, for instance, has revealed no scholarships (in the true sense) awarded while the company's promotional literature is replete with such representations. Furthermore, statements made to our office by consumers reflect that the purchase was made on the express belief that the child was to obtain some such award or belonged to some respectable organization.

While these candy companies maintain they are for profit, with no reference to charity, the very nature of the operation is couched in the aura of charitable giving to youth and could not be successful if the door-to-door salesmen were adults. It is this exploitation of young people that has promoted government agencies to use all statutory powers of regulation at their disposal.

Mr. Mulack described several abuses associated with the candy racket:

In January of this year [1974], four children, ages 8, 10, 11 and 12 years, were taken from a lower economic neighborhood after school and transported far away by a crew member to sell candy in below-freezing temperatures. After two hours of selling, the children were cold and sought to enter the auto to warm themselves, but were refused by the crew manager because they had not sold enough candy. When the children attempted to enter the auto, the crew manager physically grabbed the eleven-year-old girl by the leg and pushed her out into the snowy, wet street. The children were then informed they were "fired" and were abandoned in a strange neighborhood without money for transportation to return home.

This incident is not atypical of the complaints received by our office. In all instances the incident is caused by the child failing to sell enough candy to satisfy the crew manager. Additionally, it is not uncommon for the children to be assessed 50 cents apiece for the crew manager's gas if the children failed to reach their quota of sales.

Several reported side-effect included children at school who became disruptive and overtired in class and often fell asleep at their desks after a night of selling on the street. . . .

Carol Cochran, director of the Pennsylvania Commission on Charitable Organizations, reported an even more odious racket to the subcommittee, the National Council for Youth Endeavor (NCYE). It registered in Pennsylvania as a charitable organization designed to help mentally retarded youngsters gain meaningful employment by selling cookies and candy to the public. This "charity" was closely intertwined with another enterprise called Expedite, Inc. Both were the conceptions of Lowell Rosenjack, a resident of Cleveland, Ohio.

Ms. Cochran said Rosenjack formed Expedite, Inc.—"many years ago," he told her—and had it incorporated as a profit-making organization in Ohio. Then it began to conduct promotional drives for charity and through this got into the candy-brokerage business. As Ms. Cochran described it in her testimony, Expedite, Inc., was "using a good cause or charity as leverage for candy sales."

Late in 1971, Rosenjack formed NCYE as a nonprofit corporation in Ohio. Its goal, Ms. Cochran said, was to establish, operate, and maintain mini-workshops for the retarded and to aid in combating juvenile delinquency through the distribution of workshop products by "voluntary" junior and senior high school students. Ms. Cochran added:

Let me note here that the "workshop products" turned out to be commercially manufactured and packaged candy

—usually from Kraft—and the so-called "volunteers" were paid 25 cents per unit of candy sold.

NCYE carried out its operations in Ohio, Michigan, and Florida before coming to Pennsylvania, where it operated in the Pittsburgh and Philadelphia areas. Ms. Cochran described the operation:

> Rosenjack's procedure was to go into a community and rent a room. A minimum amount of furniture—perhaps a few tables and chairs—would be brought in. Ads would be placed in the local newspapers describing the room as a "mini-workshop" and soliciting for retarded youngsters to work there.
>
> Periodically, shipments of prepackaged candy would be delivered to the establishment. The retarded children were then supposed—after proper instruction—to affix a label to each box. The labels employed the name of the organization, National Council for Youth Endeavor, and made some mention of the product being "packaged by the handicapped."
>
> The candy was then sold door-to-door for $1.00 to $1.50 per box, depending upon the item. The actual cost of the candy varied from 35 to 38 cents per unit. The student volunteers received . . . . 25 cents per unit sold. Their drivers received 15 cents per unit of candy sold, plus 10 cents per mile driven. The retarded children—when they were paid—were to receive compensation based upon their ability to perform the tasks assigned them.

Ms. Cochran said investigation showed that the financial accounts of both NCYE and Expedite were so intertwined as to resemble "Siamese twins."

The NCYE solicitation license was revoked in Pennsylvania, and the organization was charged with operating primarily for profit under the guise of a charitable organization "and thereby creating a fraud upon the public." However, Ms. Cochran said, that was hardly stopping Rosenjack:

ANYTHING FOR KIDS

Mr. Rosenjack's latest idea is something called "Project Home Bound"—in which he would endeavor to help the handicapped at home by providing visiting monitors—high school students—who would deliver materials—no doubt more labels—to the individuals at their homes, and train them, the retarded, in arts and crafts—the arts and crafts consisting of applying certain information to pre-packaged candy. The candy, of course, would then be sold door-to-door to finance this marvelous program, in which neither the student monitors nor their subjects would receive compensation.

I say this not only with heavy sarcasm but with thinly controlled hostility as well. Because Mr. Rosenjack is *not* unique. And these cases that I've related to you today are unfortunately but two of all too many, as you [the senators] very well know . . . .

My hope is that through the information gathered in hearings like these the public will be made aware of the magnitude of the problem, and will be motivated to support—in fact, *demand*—strong legislation for the regulation of charities on a nationwide basis.

Ms. Cochran pointed out that the residents of Pennsylvania were "lucky," because it is one of the few states that has a law regulating charities and an agency to enforce it. Charity rackets are free to operate in most states, and citizens are powerless to stop them.

Candy-selling projects like these and similar rackets, can only be described as odoriferous ones at that. Two long-standing, highly regarded American principles have been corrupted. One is that it is beneficial for children and young people to have an opportunity to earn money by performing legitimate tasks, including selling. Some form of this enterprise has been going on for as long as the country has existed. In fact, there are today a number of legitimate business firms that really do employ children to sell a wide variety of items, paying them a commission on their sales. The number of youngsters who have earned money selling door to door is probably in the millions. The newspaper carrier is perhaps the outstanding example. There are also charities devoted to training young people to operate a business, make a product, and sell it for profit.

The second established principle is that children should raise money for a charity or other organization by selling something. The type of selling done by the Girl Scouts and Campfire Girls, although both of them are well organized and profitable, is only one example. Generations of American children have engaged in fund-raising efforts to benefit a school group such as the PTA or a church group or to finance a trip to Washington or some other place or to buy new band uniforms. Many legitimate purposes can be found.

There are as many methods of fund raising as human ingenuity allows. It would seem that every method has been used, from selling memberships to washing cars, from bake sales to staging plays. Some of the methods are truly novel. A band-booster club in Ohio raised a great deal of money by operating a truly scary "haunted house" one Halloween. Thousands of people paid to go through it and were appropriately frightened. Another method being used by a growing number of elementary school organizations is a balloon race. Children sell balloons house to house for 25 or 50 cents apiece. On a prescribed day, the balloons are filled with helium and tied. A tag bearing the name and address of the purchaser is attached and all are released at once. The tags returned from the farthest point win the purchasers a prize. Some organizations have hoisted more than ten thousand balloons and raised relatively large sums of money from very little effort.

The racket exposed by Senator Mondale's subcommittee corrupts both of these principles. It is one thing for a manufacturer of candy or some other item to employ children to sell to their relatives and neighbors. But it is quite another to recruit the children and then transport them by car to a strange neighborhood miles away where they are left on the street to peddle from house to house. It is one thing for a legitimate organization to raise funds for a specified purpose and a much different thing for a manufacturer to organize a phony youth charity and send off children to sell door to door in the name of nonexistent scholarships and prizes. And when the mentally retarded and other handicapped persons are brought into a scheme to line the pockets of crew managers, distributors, and manufacturers, the result is a public embarrassment that such greed exists.

The purchaser of the candy or whatever is being victimized. Even if the candy is of good quality, it is extremely overpriced. The purchaser knows this, but assumes that he is contributing to a youth club or other activity for the bedraggled tyke at the door.

But the consumer is nowhere near as victimized as the children. Persons as young as eight are transported miles from their homes and sent off to knock on doors, frequently after dark and in bad weather, to sell a product for which they receive a minuscule commission. A child may have to knock on a score or even a hundred doors to sell a single box and then be lucky at that.

In his testimony before the Senate subcommittee, Gerald Winters vehemently insisted that Youth Incentives, Inc., was benefiting ghetto youth by giving them an opportunity to earn some money. Senator Mondale pursued this point with several witnesses. At one point, he asked this question:

. . . we have heard testimony that a lot of these kids are from the ghetto and so on, and life isn't very rosy for them there, and they are coming along on these jobs, getting a chance to sell, a chance to do something, and that may not be too hot, but the alternatives aren't too hot either.

How do you respond to that?

Ms. Cochran replied:

Well, I was interested in hearing in the testimony that in the literature, one of the objects . . . of the organization was to build character, and I don't think it's building someone's good character to teach them how to rip off the public, first of all.

And certainly, you don't try to change a child's life from the ghetto—if ghetto kids are involved—through this program.

Mr. Mulack replied:

. . . If the intent of these organizations is to help that ghetto child—and I really question that intent—I say it is to use and exploit that child and to gain some sympathy from the public—then the child on the street should get more than 25 cents a box. He is the one walking up and down the neighborhoods in the cold, rainy weather; he is the one transported twenty miles across town to unfriendly territories. He's the one that does the selling, gives the sales pitch, so to speak. Twenty-five cents out of $1.50 is not helping that kid when he has to sell 10 boxes, perhaps, just to make $2.50 for that night, and to sell those 10 boxes he probably has to go to 100 or 200 homes.

Robert Green, coordinator of Charitable Solicitations for the State of Florida, said there are several programs in his state designed to aid ghetto youths. In one, the kids form a nonprofit corporation and register it with the state. They then go out to mow lawns, clean windows, and perform other jobs, for which they are paid the minimum wage. He said Florida has no objection to children earning money if the work is properly supervised, if appropriate wages are paid, and if social security and child labor laws are complied with.

Senator Mondale said he thought the United States had made a big mistake in not giving teenagers more opportunity to work, suggesting that "maybe what we have heard earlier today is the failure to provide decent alternatives" for young people.

The candy racket for "charity" hardly qualifies as an alternative.

7

To Your Good Health

Several serious questions have been raised about the operations of national health charities, including the need for them at all.

As previously discussed, the National Foundation (for Infantile Paralysis, as it was first known) was the prototype for a modern successful health charity. Basil O'Connor founded the organization and developed the techniques that made it so successful. These included the use of celebrities to raise money, heartrending portrayals of the plight of crippled children, scare tactics about the disease, and highly publicized research efforts to find a cure for the disease.

For anyone who lived during the 1940's and early 1950's, it is not possible to exaggerate the effectiveness of O'Connor's methods. Appeals on behalf of the March of Dimes were a fixture on radio. There were regular bulletins about polio outbreaks and epidemics. New cases were reported daily in newspapers. Mothers were warned not to let their children swim in community pools at various times. Other precautions were recommended. The symptoms of the disease were constantly reported until parents were in a state of panic if a child ran a fever or had a stiff neck or sore muscles.* In short, O'Connor made polio seem a very real threat to Americans.

One cannot exaggerate either the sense of national pride or the relief that was felt when polio was finally conquered in 1955 with the vaccine developed by Dr. Jonas Salk. The milestones along the way were the discovery that polio was carried by a virus—actually by three different virus strains—the isolation of the virus, the discovery that the virus was carried by the bloodstream. With this information, development of a suitable vaccine became a foregone conclusion.†

The Salk vaccine had an electrifying effect on Americans. Here was the finest evidence that American charity, when combined with American scientific know-how, could eliminate all the diseases that afflict mankind. Health charities have seldom let the American giver forget

---

*For a brief period in 1950–51, I worked as an orderly in the Children's Hospital of the State University of Iowa in Iowa City. The hospital received polio victims from all over the state. My job was to carry the patients to and from physical therapy and to assist in physical therapy. The treatment consisted of applying steaming towels to the affected limbs, followed by exhaustive physical therapy and hydrotherapy. The idea was to keep the muscles from atrophying so they would still function in the event the child recovered from the disease enough to permit their use. In its early stages, polio was extremely painful. The courage of the suffering young patients was both inspiring and unforgettable.

†There has long been a bit of a flap about that in the scientific community, because some scientists feel that Dr. Salk's work was technical in nature and fairly routine. In short, some jealousy developed over his celebrity status when those who had paved the way for his work remained unrecognized and forgotten.

this idea. A host of health charities have been created to find miracle cures for other diseases, both the well-known kind and the obscure.

Some questions were raised about the polio campaign at the time and they have continued since then. By extension, the same questions are being asked about the other and newer health charities. For starters, the incidence of polio was never particularly high. It was certainly far less a cause of death than cancer, heart disease, and accidents. Statistically, the most common disease in America is mental illness. Some say that half the hospital beds in the nation are used by the mentally ill. Yet mental-health groups have great difficulty raising funds.

By far the most common affliction of children is mental retardation. But fund raising to combat mental retardation and to care for the mentally retarded lags far behind that of relatively obscure diseases.

The complaint was made about polio that the scare tactics and heartrending appeals to raise funds distorted health care as a whole in America. A disproportionate share of the charity health dollar was channeled into this single program and other diseases were neglected.

The complaint was also made that the National Foundation did not always spend its polio funds wisely. O'Connor was president of both the National Foundation and the Georgia Warm Springs Foundation, a small, one-hundred-bed regional hospital where President Roosevelt went for treatment. Between 1938 and 1958, the National Foundation headquarters gave Warm Springs $5 million and individual foundation chapters gave it another $10 million. Many thought this particularly generous for such a small facility, many of whose patients were self-supporting and paid their own way.

There was also a good bit of discussion about O'Connor

investing $500,000 in 1956 in a study of what the National Foundation should do after polio was cured, as well as a lot of speculation about the size of O'Connor's expense account. How much he received was never revealed.

The most criticism was leveled at O'Connor's pet program to develop gamma globulin as a polio preventative. In 1951 and 1952 the Foundation gave $500,000 to investigate the blood derivative as a preventative. Tests showed gamma globulin not very effective for this purpose. Nevertheless, in 1953, O'Connor spent $5 million to buy up gamma globulin and another $500,000 for a machine to manufacture it. In 1956, when the Salk vaccine was already in production, O'Connor spent another $9 million for gamma globulin. Critics assumed that the National Foundation had collected more money than it could spend in the polio fight and was just spending the excess in any way it could.*

Another criticism of the National Foundation is that it didn't go out of business when its polio fight succeeded. Many argue that the manpower, experience, and reputation of the organization should have been utilized for a new charitable purpose. In any event, the foundation was faced with a difficult problem when it elected to stay in operation. Most of the major and quite a few of the minor disorders were already represented by established health charities. For a time the National Foundation seemed to be a charity in search of a cause.

The problem was solved when the foundation chose birth defects. A great many children are born blind, deaf, diseased, or crippled or deformed in some way. Some

---

*This is a rather common problem of nonprofit organizations. It is obviously important at year's end not to have excess funds. Such organizations frequently launch "educational" programs or themselves donate to charity so as to maintain their nonprofit status.

defects result from poor prenatal care or accidents at birth, but many are hereditary in nature. A new area of medical research has developed in which doctors hope to understand the causes of birth defects, learn to predict when such defects might occur, and perhaps discover how to prevent them by altering genetic instruction—surely a frontier of medicine and biology. This was the field the National Foundation entered, notwithstanding the fact that other charities working with the blind, deaf, crippled, and mentally retarded were also interested in these matters.

Another example of a charity that outlived its cause was what used to be called the American Tuberculosis Association. Tuberculosis was a world-wide scourge for centuries. The illness was grave, and recovery in a sanatorium took a long time. Raising funds through the sale of Christmas seals, the Tuberculosis Association did excellent work in educating the public, caring for diseased patients, and financing research into a cure. In the 1950's, various "miracle" drugs were developed that greatly speeded recovery from the disease and lowered the incidence of it. Programs of chest X rays were launched to encourage early diagnosis, and a patch test was developed that also aided in diagnosis. A vaccine was developed and used around the world, though not (for reasons that many think inexplicable) in the United States. By the mid-1960's, tuberculosis had ceased to be the pestilence it once was, although it has not been wiped out entirely. Detection and cure are simply far easier.

Nonetheless, the American Tuberculosis Association kept on selling Christmas seals and raising funds to fight tuberculosis. In time, the Association branched out into other respiratory diseases and then changed its name to the American Lung Association. It still supports tuberculosis patients, but its most visible activity is preparing TV commercials that warn against cigarette smoking as a cause of lung cancer and emphysema.

Considerable overlap exists among the health agencies, the conflict between the National Foundation and other charities over birth defects being only one example. The American Cancer Society is by far our largest health charity. Yet the Lung Association, as we have seen, is concerned with lung cancer, too. Then there is the Leukemia Society of America, which was organized in 1949 with forty-four chapters nationwide. Another name for leukemia is cancer of the blood. There are the Damon Runyon-Walter Winchell Cancer Fund and the United Cancer Council, based in Indianapolis and serving twenty-seven million people. Funds working with kidney, liver, and other diseases have to cope with cancer patients, too, and of course the Easter Seal Society is interested in cancer as a crippler of children. We must likewise assume that the Easter Seal Society becomes involved with patients who suffer from arthritis, muscular dystrophy, multiple sclerosis, and similar diseases for which national fund-raising organizations already exist.

But such conflicts of interest pale beside the overlap between the health charities and the federal government. When the National Foundation was fighting polio in the 1940's and early 1950's, it did so almost alone. Federal expenditures for polio or any other type of medical research were nil, or nearly so. But with the success of the polio campaign and the shock of the Russians' successful launching of Sputnik in 1957, thus beating America in the space race, the federal government began to spend vast sums of money on all types of research, including medical research. A dozen agencies, notably the Department of Defense and the National Institutes of Health (part of the

Department of Health, Education, and Welfare), receive billions of dollars a year, appropriated by a generous Congress, to spend on medical research.

Some problems have resulted. As a hallmark of his administration, President Nixon declared a war on cancer, an all-out drive to conquer the disease. Congress responded with billions of dollars. A great deal of research was performed and progress made, yet a preventative or cure for cancer remains highly elusive. Cancer is far more complex than polio is. Cancer is not one disease but several, and it may have many causes and need many cures. Too, understanding the causes and cures for cancer seems to involve understanding the most elementary processes of life, including the human cell in all its variety, its genetic instruction, sustenance, and reproduction. Cancer researchers are often working at the absolute frontier between man's knowledge and lack of it. Some scientists are saying that no amount of money and effort is likely to produce a cure for cancer soon, and that a disservice has been done to the public because it has been misled into believing that the simple expenditure of money can conquer the disease.

More to the point of this book is the question of the role of private charities, such as the American Cancer Society, in such a gigantic government effort. Even the $97 million a year raised by the society is tiny compared to the government's billions of dollars. To some critics, it seems that Americans are paying taxes to support governmental medical research and then contributing to health charities that have the same purpose. It is argued that private charities ought to confine themselves to areas neglected by the government rather than add to such a behemoth exercise as cancer research.

There is an answer for these critics. The health charities

do far more than spend money for research. They perform important tasks of public education about disease and its symptoms and care. They enlist the support of millions of volunteers who become interested in the disease and work on behalf of the victims. The charity becomes a means to involve large numbers of people in the medical program and thereby bring more human ingenuity to the program than government bureaucrats do. If health charities have sometimes wasted money on fruitless research, they have also encouraged innovative or neglected areas of research to the advantage of all.

In short, relatively few people want medical research and health care to be left solely in government hands. Most of us feel that something peculiarly American would be lost if private giving disappeared from the health field. Indeed, a number of Western European countries with more comprehensive public health programs are trying to find ways to increase the activities of private charities.

Another criticism of the health charities is that they distort the nation's real health needs. The following table shows the amounts raised through contributions and bequests by leading health agencies in 1975:

American Cancer Society	$97,268,935
American Heart Association	58,920,969
The National Foundation (birth defects)	48,699,950
American Lung Association	40,171,905
National Easter Seal Society for Crippled Children and Adults	37,800,000*
Muscular Dystrophy Associations of America	27,090,340
National Association for Retarded Citizens	23,975,000
Planned Parenthood Federation of America	20,000,000*
United Cerebral Palsy Association	19,653,147*
National Association for Mental Health	14,760,000*
National Multiple Sclerosis Society	13,721,282
The Arthritis Foundation	10,790,200*

TO YOUR GOOD HEALTH

Cystic Fibrosis Foundation	8,400,000*
Leukemia Society of America	7,531,375
National Kidney Foundation	6,000,000*
Epilepsy Foundation of America	4,024,552
National Society for the Prevention of Blindness	3,648,418
National Council on Alcoholism	3,500,000*
American Foundation for the Blind	3,172,641
National Hemophilia Foundation	2,982,795
American Diabetes Association	2,552,200*
Damon Runyon-Walter Winchell Cancer Fund	2,020,000
Recording for the Blind	1,397,682

*Estimate

Source: *Giving USA* for 1975, published by the American Association of Fund-Raising Counsel.

(The reader may compare this table with that on page 48 to observe the changes in some of these charities' fortunes. Note the increase in National Foundation contributions and the decrease in the National Easter Seal Society, for example. Lung and Muscular Dystrophy both grew.)

As the above table shows, the American Cancer Society alone raises nearly half again as much more money ($97 million to $58 million) as the American Heart Association. Yet diseases of the heart and blood vessels (cardiovascular disease) kill almost three times as many Americans each year as cancer, the second leading cause of death. Based upon official government figures on the causes of death, our third-largest health fund might be called "the National Society for the Prevention of Accidents."

Of our major health charities, only two others deal with diseases that cause a significant number of deaths in the United States. They are the American Lung Association, which raises funds for emphysema and bronchitis, and the American Diabetes Association. The list of causes of death in the United States follows:

Cause of Death	No. of Deaths	Rate per 100,000 Population
Cardiovascular Disease	1,073,460	494.4
Cancer	353,440	168.4
Accidents	115,040	54.8
Influenza and pneumonia	61,160	29.1
Ill-defined conditions	38,310	18.3
Diabetes	36,450	17.4
Cirrhosis of liver	33,630	16.0
Certain causes of infant mortality	31,030	14.8
Bronchitis, emphysema, and asthma	30,280	14.4
Suicide	24,440	11.6
Homicide	19,700	9.4
Congenital anomalies	13,940	6.6

No other cause of death exceeded 10,000 deaths or a death rate of more than 5 out of every 100,000 persons.

If they based their efforts solely on the causes of death in the United States, the private charities might be better off raising funds on behalf of pneumonia, cirrhosis of the liver, and unexplained infant deaths, not to mention accidents, suicides, and murders, rather than for such obscure killers as arthritis, muscular dystrophy, cystic fibrosis, multiple sclerosis, epilepsy, and hemophilia, to name a few.

The nature of our giving is hard to understand. Why is so much more money given to fight cancer than heart disease? Both affect the young as well as the elderly. In fact, about twice as many children die of cardiovascular disease as do of cancer. The number of children dying from heart disease is less than 100,000 fewer than all persons, adults and children, dying from cancer. We gave $37 million to the Easter Seal Society on behalf of crippled children and $48 million to the National Foundation to

fight birth defects and $27 million for muscular dys-
trophy, while the American Diabetes Association, which
is trying to combat a proven killer of more than 36,000
people a year, can raise only $2.5 million.

Of course, you might say that it is unfair to cite causes of
death as a judgment of the worth of a charity. Crippled
children may live with the affliction their entire lives.
Arthritis seldom kills anyone, yet it causes years of pain
and deformity. Muscular dystrophy and multiple sclerosis are slow incapacitators of people. A diabetic lives for
years with a need for medication, restricted activity, and
special diet. Childbirth is a particular risk to diabetic
women. Cirrhosis of the liver is certainly an unpleasant
way to die. Peptic ulcers, which kill twice as many people
as tuberculosis, bring a life of constant pain to the afflicted. If the point has not yet been made, consider the
lifetimes of suffering endured by the mentally retarded
and the mentally ill.

It is not being argued here that one health charity is
"better" than another and that therefore one ought to give
to Heart and not to Cancer, or to Diabetes and not to
Arthritis. Far from it. The point is that health priorities are
distorted. The success of a charity sometimes depends
more upon the success of its fund-raising appeals—its
advertising, fund-raising methods, celebrity backing,
management efficiency—than the true urgency of the
cause.

A perusal of the causes of death raises the question of
whether health charities distort the prevalence of a particular disease, as well as their own efforts to combat it.
Certainly some of them have ever since Basil O'Connor
summarily spent $8.1 million in 1958 on "epidemic aid"
when only 6,000 cases of polio (compared to perhaps
30,000 cases in some years) were reported.

Senator Mondale's subcommittee sought to investigate this matter of charity distortion by questioning officers of the Epilepsy Foundation of America. As charities go in the health field, it is a diminutive one, raising a little over $4 million in a recent year. The epilepsy organization had come under fire because of its high fund-raising costs. A third of all the money collected went to raise the money. The Epilepsy Foundation also had the highest management costs—15 percent of the donations—of any charity belonging to the National Health Council. Thus, 48 percent of the money given went for fund raising and operating the charity.

The subcommittee had hired as its consultant Harvey Katz, author of the book *Give! Who Gets Your Charity Dollar?* Mr. Katz had made a particular study of the Epilepsy Foundation and had reported on it in unfavorable terms. He had found a strangely high turnover of the charity's executives. In one year, the EFA had paid more than $30,000 to employment agencies to recruit executives, many of whom stayed only a few weeks or months. Mr. Katz blamed the personnel problems on the management style of Paul E. Funk, the executive vice president. According to Mr. Katz, Mr. Funk took even minor decisions into his own hands and was slow to make them. This left subordinates frustrated in their jobs.

When the subcommittee questioned Mr. Funk about the high management costs, he explained them on the basis that EFA was a new organization. It was having trouble getting the right personnel and was spending a great deal of effort and money in organizing its local chapters.

The high fund-raising costs were of concern both to Mr. Funk and the National Health Council, and they were attributed to the EFA's use of the so-called "penny letter."

A fund-raising gimmick had been started some years before of attaching a shiny new penny to the solicitation letter. The appeal for funds was built around the gift of this penny to the potential donor. Use of the penny was frowned on by the National Health Council, which considers it unethical for a charity to send any unsolicited merchandise to potential givers. Furthermore, the penny letter greatly increased the cost of each letter mailed and thus of fund raising. EFA bore the cost of the penny and the cost of attaching it to the letter and paying the postage on it.

Both Mr. Funk and Arthur J. Grimes, who spoke for the National Health Council, expressed a desire to eliminate the penny letter as a fund-raising technique. But every time the penny was dropped from the solicitation, contributions diminished.

Neither Mr. Katz in his book nor the Senate subcommittee raised the pertinent question of whether a charity on behalf of epilepsy ought to exist at all. It is reasonable to ask what purpose the charity serves other than to spend forty-eight cents of the contributor's dollar in raising funds and managing the national headquarters.

The term "epilepsy" is a modern one used to describe persons who suffer from periodic convulsions or seizures or, as they used to be called, "fits." In a serious seizure, the person loses consciousness, muscles of the body go rigid, and there is associated writhing. In severe cases, the person might incur injury. The muscle spasms are so severe that limbs are sometimes broken, and first aid is necessary to prevent the patient from falling and hurting himself. One should also insert an object between the teeth of a person having a seizure so the tongue won't be bitten. Most patients, although not all, come out of the seizure naturally after a few minutes. They generally do not know what happened and are extremely fatigued. The frequency and severity of seizures vary widely. Some are so slight that even the victim does not know he has had one. There are types of seizures that last only a few seconds and the victim may have many of them a day. Neurologists now recognize such seizures as a cause of learning disabilities in children.

Because of the nature of seizures, ancient man attached great superstition to them. They were said to be the work of evil spirits or the devil. Until quite recent times, people who had seizures were subject to ridicule. Parents kept afflicted children home from school and often hid them from view. Laws restricting the activities of people affected thus still exist. They may not obtain a driver's license, for example.

In the last quarter century, a great deal of medical research has been done on the causes of seizures. Doctors now understand better why they occur and have greatly improved methods for treating convulsions and preventing them altogether. Convulsions have many causes. Drugs will sometimes cause them. Many children will convulse during a high fever. Indeed, convulsions can be induced. A long-standing treatment for the mentally ill has been to induce seizures by administering an electric shock to the brain. This treatment is supposed to affect the patient's short-term memory, perhaps eradicating the cause of the emotional disorders. Electroshock therapy has always been controversial. It used to be administered routinely and without anesthetic, causing great pain to the patient. Electroshock is now used sparingly in mental hospitals. When it is done at all, the patient is given an anesthetic and muscle relaxants are used to control the seizures.

A tendency toward seizures can readily be identified by an electroencephalogram (EEG) or the measuring of electrical activity in the brain. The tendency shows up as a marked pattern, frequently called a "spike," in the brain waves—although some persons have the spike and never have a seizure.

Fewer physicians today use the word *epilepsy* than ever before. They believe there is no such thing as a disease by that name. Rather, they see the seizures as symptoms of various neurological disorders.

Persons who have seizures are now routinely treated with drugs, notably a barbiturate such as phenobarbital or a medication marketed under the name Dilantin. With correct dosage, most seizures can be prevented in two thirds to three quarters of the patients, and they can live a normal life. It is also recognized that many children tend to stop having seizures as they reach their teens.

If epilepsy is being discounted as a disease and patients are being routinely treated by drugs, it becomes a little difficult to understand the need for the Epilepsy Foundation of America. Perhaps there is need for public education to break down any lingering superstitions about persons who have convulsions. The EFA spends 9 percent of its funds for this purpose. Doctors routinely treat persons with seizures, most of whom lead normal lives under medication. Rarely does one see a person having a convulsion in public. Therefore, it is difficult to understand why 5 percent of the EFA's money needs to go for "professional education."

Of course, more research into the causes of seizures may be necessary, and better drugs might be developed. Perhaps seizures could be prevented without the use of drugs. The EFA has an interest in such research. In a recent year, it spent four cents of every donated dollar for research.

The Senate subcommittee heard testimony challenging the research claims of the EFA. In its fund-raising letter, the EFA said that "grants from Epilepsy Foundation of America right now are supporting long-range research which may finally lead to a cure for epilepsy." Another EFA document spoke of important research being performed by Dr. Reginald G. Bickford at the University of California at San Diego. He and his associates were developing a system to make diagnosis of seizures through EEG's easier. The EFA claimed that "the system has been developed under an EFA grant."

Investigation showed that the EFA had granted $900 to Robert R. Meyers to continue his work with Dr. Bickford on a summer fellowship. The great bulk of Dr. Bickford's work had been financed by four grants from the National Institutes of Health totaling $394,261. The EFA's contribution had been minimal, hardly justifying a claim to have financed development of the new diagnostic system.

Other claims in EFA promotional literature were disputed. The subcommittee heard testimony from Dr. John F. Kurtzke, professor of Neurology at Georgetown University in Washington, and Dr. Donald Harting, former Director of the National Institute of Child Health and Human Development. Both doctors attacked EFA promotional literature as "self-serving" on several grounds. For example, EFA literature spoke of 4 million people afflicted with epilepsy. Drs. Kurtzke and Harting testified that a more generally accepted figure is about 1 million afflicted persons.

The witnesses also attacked a statement from an EFA brochure entitled "Epilepsy is America's Concern" that "it is America's concern because epilepsy affects more Americans than cancer, tuberculosis, cerebral palsy, muscular dystrophy, and multiple sclerosis *combined*."

The two doctors described how this statement was justified. There are two ways to report statistics on the frequency of a disease. One is the *incidence*, that is, the number of *new* cases reported each year. The other is the *prevalence*, that is, the total of new, continuing, and chronic cases within the population. These figures are usually reported as so many cases per 100,000 or 1 million population. Obviously, the incidence—that is, new cases—is usually a lower figure than the prevalence, which is all existing cases.

Drs. Kurtzke and Harting suggested that in arriving at the statement above, the EFA reported the low incidence figures for cancer, TB, cerebral palsy, muscular dystrophy, and multiple sclerosis, and the prevalence figure for epilepsy. Had all incidence or all prevalence figures been used, the results would have been very different. They also suggested that it was unfair to compare a generally nonfatal condition such as epilepsy with a fatal disease such as cancer. Even the prevalence figures for cancer are kept low because so many victims die each year.

EFA promotional literature was also attacked for overstating the cost of the malady. In a fact sheet about epilepsy, distributed by EFA, the cost of drug treatment was placed at about $500 a year. Dr. Harting estimated the yearly cost of Dilantin at no more than $70 a year. He based this estimate on figures supplied by the other major epilepsy charity, the National Epilepsy League of Chicago, which dispenses about $350,000 worth of therapeutic drugs a year at a cost per person of $35 to $40 a year. The $70 figure was the estimated cost were a patient to buy the same amount of Dilantin in the drugstore.

The EFA fact sheet made no mention of the availability of low-cost drugs from the National Epilepsy League or the money made available for these purposes from state and federal funds to aid crippled children. Dr. Harting added:

I am simply making the point . . . that by omitting one of the major groups that does provide services on a national basis to people with epilepsy, it seems to me that these omissions indicate that this information sheet is another promotional document for the Epilepsy Foundation of America rather than a competent and unbiased compilation of useful facts for persons with epilepsy.

It is perhaps unfortunate that the EFA was singled out for these inquiries by the Senate subcommittee. Chances are that the EFA is no better or worse run than other health charities. It may be typical or it may be exceptional. No one knows for sure.

Ever since the debut of Basil O'Connor and the National Foundation in 1938, health charities have tended to overstate the prevalence of a particular disease, the horrors of it, the high cost of treating it, and the efforts of the charity to combat it, particularly in the area of research. Dr. Kurtzke drew laughter by reporting that "an epidemologist from Harvard presented a paper postulating that by taking the voluntary agency claims, every individual in the country was affected with at least two diseases."

The point was made that the contributing public is rather helpless when confronted with high and conflicting claims for the prevalence of disease, because very few reliable figures are available on the incidence and prevalence of various diseases. A charity finds it easy to take a very high figure to justify its needs for donations, for it is difficult for even the expert, let alone the average contributor, to dispute the claims. Drs. Harting and Kurtzke suggested that either a private or public agency be charged with responsibility to provide reliable information on the incidence, prevalence, and cost of various diseases so accurate information could reach the public.

8

When the Rich Die

An old adage maintains that "you can't take it with you," meaning that a person's money has no value in the grave, or in heaven or hell, as the case may be. In the United States, the next best thing to taking it with you is to create a foundation to spend your money as you would like to long after you are gone.

In a recent year the United States had an estimated 26,000 foundations controlling assets—stocks, bonds, land, buildings, corporations—worth over $34 billion. Of this total, 2,533 foundations were considered large—that is, they had assets of more than $1 million. These large foundations dominate the field, possessing $31.5 billion in assets, compared to a mere $2.6 billion for the remaining 22,421 foundations. Indeed, a person need not be wealthy to create a foundation. Nearly half the foundations, 12,681 of them, have assets of less than $50,000.

A foundation is a nonprofit organization created to

spend or give away the income from its assets and sometimes the assets themselves for a philanthropic purpose. That can be just about any purpose—education, health, public welfare, maintenance of homes and memorials, various types of study or research. Just about any individual, family, corporation, or even an entire community can create and fund a foundation. A foundation can either exist solely on the bequest of its original founder, or its assets can be increased by relatives or even total strangers who agree with its purpose.

The nation's foundations made gifts, usually termed grants, totaling $2.11 billion in a recent year. This is a large sum, yet it represents only 8.4 percent of the total amount given away that year in the United States. It exceeds the 4.7 percent from corporations, about equals the 8.2 percent derived from bequests to specific charities, but is dwarfed by the 78.7 percent given by individuals.

Of the $2.11 billion, 28 percent went for education, 20 percent for health, 16 percent for welfare, 12 percent for the sciences, 11 percent each to international projects and American humanities, and 2 percent for religious purposes. This level of giving by foundations represented 7.1 percent of foundation assets, a sharp increase over the 4 to 5 percent of assets given in previous years.

The increase in the percentage of giving in relation to assets reflects the sharp drop in the value of foundation assets brought about by the decline in the stock market, as well as by the expenditure of assets. The Ford Foundation, the largest in the nation, recently reported assets of $1.8 billion, which was about half the assets it reported in 1968. The Rockefeller Foundation assets declined from $890 million in 1968 to $619.5 million at the end of 1974. The Duke Endowment (based on the American Tobacco Company fortune) declined in the same period from $629 million to about $250 million; the Carnegie Corporation of New York from $334 million to just under $200 million; the Danforth Foundation (Purina Corporation) from $173 million to $38 million; and the John A. Hartford Foundation (A & P Company) from $352 million to under $102 million. A few companies grew in assets during the period, notably the Lilly Foundation (pharmaceuticals) which almost doubled from $579 million to just over $1 billion.

The role of foundations in American philanthropy is complex if only because so many foundations exist, each with a different origin, history, purpose, and record of accomplishment. At best their accomplishments can be described as uneven, ranging from brilliant contributions to the nation and the world to what amounts to no more than a deliberate rip-off of the public treasury.

Foundations have long been controversial in America. From their inception shortly after the turn of the century, many people have objected to their very existence. In the context of the time, it seemed that a foundation represented the accumulation of wealth by "robber barons" who had become rich by price gouging, monopolistic business practices, and often even sacrificing their employees to their ambition. That this individual was now giving money to charity did not alter, in the eyes of many, the fact that it was tainted money.

An example of the public distrust of foundations came in 1910 when a bill was introduced in the Senate to authorize the formation of the Rockefeller Foundation. John D. Rockefeller, Sr., did not need a legislative sanction for his foundation, but he sought one, perhaps because he wanted public approval of his generosity.

Probably more than any other individual of the time, Rockefeller symbolized the robber baron. His Standard Oil companies not only controlled nearly all the nation's oil but had pioneered many of the monopolistic practices adopted by less ingenious industrialists. His atrocities against his workers were notorious. All of this was brought up at the Senate hearings on the bill. His proposed foundation was viewed as "an indefinite scheme for perpetuating great wealth." The Senate never did pass the bill, but the New York legislature incorporated the foundation and it went into operation in 1913.

There have been repeated investigations of foundations, most recently in 1969, when Congress passed new laws restricting their activities and for the first time taxing them. Public attitudes toward foundations today range from respect for their accomplishments and a desire to encourage them, to the belief that they are anachronistic and not very useful organizations that should be eradicated. Foundations are criticized both for being moribund, conservative, and unimaginative in dealing with national problems, and for being too liberal, even radical, in funding social and educational programs.

We can enter this thicket of controversy by briefly examining a few of the foundations, not necessarily the largest or best known but those representing various types of foundations, their activities, and their problems.

Andrew Carnegie came to the United States penniless from Scotland and built the Carnegie Steel Corporation into the world's largest. In 1901, he had sold the company for $250 million in bonds—a stupendous sum even now but gigantic in those days. Carnegie Steel became the United States Steel Company, still the world's largest.

Thereafter, Carnegie devoted himself to philanthropy. It is said he spent the last thirty years of his life giving away the fortune he amassed in the first fifty. He wrote and lectured on the virtues of philanthropy, the evils of wealth, and the need for brotherhood among men, although he had permitted the slaughter of his workers in a series of bloody strikes.

Carnegie's personal philanthropy was impressive. He gave away $43 million to establish more than two thousand libraries; he created the Carnegie Institution of Pittsburgh as a museum and the Carnegie Institute of Technology (now Carnegie-Mellon University) with gifts totaling $12 million; he gave $10 million to Scottish universities; he created the Carnegie Institute of Washington, D.C., with a grant of $12 million to do basic research in science; he gave $5 million for a fund to recognize heroic deeds by civilians; he established the Carnegie Foundation for the Advancement of Teaching with a $10 million grant and thereby made an invaluable contribution to higher education by creating an insurance fund for educators; he also founded the Carnegie Endowment for International Peace with $10 million.

In 1911, Carnegie established the Carnegie Corporation of New York, which still functions as a leading foundation. The Carnegie foundation is not only the nation's oldest, but in the view of many it is probably the best. It employs an excellent professional staff and has had several highly regarded men as its president. Through the years, its primary interest has been in the field of education. The foundation did much to encourage adult education and to improve both the quantity and quality of higher education. In more recent years, it has sought to improve the quality of primary and secondary education, particularly for disadvantaged youths, and in general to deal with the problems of ghetto residents.

Some of the Carnegie Corporation's more recent grants have gone to support experimental high schools to assist dropouts, to finance community law offices to help ghetto residents obtain their legal rights, to support a training program for medical personnel to work among urban and rural poor, and with the Ford Foundation to finance the Children's Television Workshop to produce new types of television shows for children. The acclaimed *Sesame Street* program is an outgrowth of that endeavor.

The Rockefeller family has been engaged in major philanthropy for four generations. The Rockefeller Foundation is the largest of the family charities, and the Rockefeller Brothers Fund is perhaps next in size with assets well into nine figures. The latter was founded in 1940 by the five grandsons of John D. Rockefeller, Sr.: Vice President Nelson A. Rockefeller, Laurence Rockefeller, David Rockefeller, who is chairman of the Chase Manhattan Bank, one of the nation's largest, John D. Rockefeller III, and the late Winthrop Rockefeller, former governor of Arkansas. Other members of the family have contributed to these two funds, as well as created other foundations. All in all, there are perhaps a dozen Rockefeller foundations.

With so much money being given away for so many years, it is not even possible to list the Rockefeller philanthropic activities in a short space. Suffice it to say that the Rockefeller fortune has been put to some outstanding uses. The Rockefellers have been major benefactors of the fine arts, conservation, and higher education. The Rockefeller Brothers Fund, in particular, has been interested in African and Latin American affairs, and it has been generous with a number of black colleges, various black civil-rights leaders, and the National Urban League.

Perhaps the most notable achievements of the family philanthropy, especially of the Rockefeller Foundation, have been in the areas of medical and scientific research. It is only a slight exaggeration to say that a list of the recipients of Rockefeller grants might be entitled "Who's

Who in Science" or "Nobel Laureates We Have Known"
or even "What's What in Science." Rockefeller money has
led to yellow-fever vaccine and control of malaria, the
theoretical basis for the atomic bomb and nuclear power,
and the so-called green revolution to ease world hunger. It
has fostered the study of world population, financed research into birth control, founded and funded medical
schools and scientific facilities the world over, and made
direct outlays to combat health problems at home and
abroad. The Rockefeller Foundation is criticized for being
less than innovative in dealing with social problems, but
its efforts in support of medicine, health, and science have
often been exemplary.

The Ford Foundation was organized in 1936 from the
fortune of Henry Ford, the auto magnate. But "old Henry"
left his company in such a state of disarray that a number
of years elapsed before the company could recover and
become the profitable corporation it is today. Henry Ford
II, grandson of the founder, is credited with that industrial metamorphosis. Not until 1951 did "young Henry"
give his attention to the affairs of the foundation. Before
that the foundation was not particularly prosperous, because most of its assets were in Ford Motor Company
stock. When the company began to make money, so did
the foundation.

The Ford Foundation has always been plagued with
controversy, which has stemmed in part from its close
relationship with the auto company. The foundation was,
in fact, the principal owner of the company, and even
though its shares were classified as "nonvoting"—that is,
it had no voice in company affairs—that did not mean, at
least in the eyes of the public, that the company had no say
in foundation affairs. Indeed, "young Henry" has long
been active in foundation decisions. Even when the

foundation sold off many of its company shares to the public and used the money to diversify its holdings, the relationship between the company and the foundation remained suspect.

Controversy has surrounded the men chosen to head the foundation, too. The first president was Paul G. Hoffman, who had administered the Marshall Plan of postwar aid to Europe. He was active in Republican politics and, while he was foundation president, supported the campaign of President Eisenhower. As foundation president he gave free rein to Robert M. Hutchins, then chancellor of the University of Chicago, who was an outspoken advocate of highly controversial educational policies. When the foundation generously supported him, controversy followed. Even the current president, McGeorge Bundy, is unacceptable to many because of his role in the Vietnam War as adviser to Presidents Kennedy and Johnson.

The foundation has undertaken many programs, as befits its great wealth. In the mid-1960's, it was spending as much as $365 million a year, but since then it has curtailed its outlays to about $200 million a year. Its major grants have been to colleges, universities, medical schools, and hospitals, and those grants have been prodigious. In 1955, it gave $260 million to over 600 private colleges to increase faculty salaries, $198 million to 3,500 hospitals to improve their services, and $90 million to 45 medical schools.

Much of this money was dispensed with little regard for selectivity. At the meeting where the grants to medical schools were approved, Henry Ford II is alleged to have remarked, "Let's make the total an uneven number—perhaps ninety-one million point something—so it will look like we have considered the matter carefully." In 1965, the foundation pointed with pride to having dispensed $900 million in grants to universities. In recent years, the foundation has diversified its program of grants, but it is still heavily committed to education and national affairs.

One of the largest and wealthiest families in the nation is the Du Pont family. Profits from its chemical and other businesses have gone into more than a score of foundations. The two largest are the Longwood Foundation, established in 1937, and the Nemours Foundation, established in 1936.

The Longwood Foundation has as its principal purpose, according to the will of Pierre S. du Pont, the "support, operation and development of the Longwood gardens near Kennett Square, Pennsylvania." Suffice it to say, the Longwood Gardens, the largest group of formal gardens in the world, are a horticultural showplace. They are open to the public year round.

The Foundation has also made grants to various institutions in the Philadelphia area, including $1.8 million to Swarthmore College and $1 million to predominantly black Lincoln University.

The Nemours Foundation was established by Alfred I. du Pont. Its purpose was to see that his wife received the income from his wealth during her lifetime, after which the foundation was to maintain the Alfred I. du Pont Estate, although at no point was it to interfere in the operation of the estate.

Mrs. du Pont lived until 1970, receiving over $100 million in income from the foundation. The other principal activity of the foundation was to build and operate a children's hospital in Delaware. It treats about two thousand patients annually.

The foundation receives most of its money from the Du Pont estate in Florida, which is known locally as "the empire." Until forced by the federal government to divest itself of some of them, the estate controlled thirty banks in

Florida, one of which, the Jacksonville National Bank, controlled over $1 billion in trust accounts. The estate also controls the St. Joe Paper Company, which owns more than a million acres of woodland in Florida and Georgia and is one of the nation's largest. The estate held more than 700,000 shares of Du Pont chemical stock and over 400,000 shares of General Motors. Its assets were estimated at over $1 billion a few years ago.

The relationship between the foundation and the Du Pont estate has been scrutinized repeatedly. It is hard to see the charitable gains from this great wealth, for relatively little of the estate's earnings have gone for any philanthropic purpose.

The Lilly Foundation, now the nation's third largest,* with assets of over $1 billion, was formed in 1937 by the Lilly family, owners of a pharmaceutical house in Indianapolis, Indiana. The Lilly Foundation has long been controlled by members of the Lilly family with a small professional staff. Its activities have been primarily confined, although not exclusively, to the Indiana and Indianapolis area. Many local education, welfare, and cultural organizations have benefited from the Lilly Foundation, and the family has also had a pronounced interest in two other philanthropic activities, religion of a fundamentalist theology and right-wing patriotic and anti-Communist causes. The foundation has never developed a coherent program for spending its vast resources, other than to avoid gifts in the health field because of its relationship to the family business.

---

*Second rank behind the Ford Foundation is held by the Robert Wood Johnson Foundation, based upon the wealth of the Johnson & Johnson Company, makers of surgical dressings. It was founded in 1936, but operated on a very limited basis until it received more than $1 billion upon the death of its founder in 1968. It is active in the health field.

In his book *The Big Foundations* (Columbia University Press, 1972) Waldemar A. Nielsen summed up the Lilly Foundation in these words:

> To the great loss of the troubled city of Indianapolis and the surrounding region, the endowment remains a mediocre and incoherent philanthropy—major only in its resources.

The Houston Endowment, with assets of over $100 million, illustrates the complexities of managing large foundations. It was formed in 1937 by Jesse Jones, who served as Secretary of Commerce under Franklin D. Roosevelt. Prior to his death in 1956, Jones became known as "Mr. Houston" for his many contributions to the Texas city. He was a very wealthy man, owning real estate, hotels, corporations, a major newspaper (the Houston *Chronicle*), banks, and insurance companies. With Jones's death, the Houston Endowment came to possess controlling shares in twenty-six separate corporations, most of them based in Houston.

The directors of the foundation have been understandably busy operating these twenty-six corporations on a profitable basis. The officers of the corporations all report directly to the foundation's directors, who, equally understandably, have great importance in the economic well-being of Houston and environs. Most of the Houston Endowment's grants ($10 million in 1974) have gone to educational, cultural, and charitable institutions in or near Houston. Among its notable grants have been a scholarship program for Houston high-school seniors and several million dollars for a performing-arts center for the city.

Out of many foundations, these few perhaps represent the virtues, faults, and problems of all foundations as philanthropic organizations.

An evaluation of them can begin with the reasons for their formation. The early ones, such as the Carnegie and the Rockefeller, were formed back in an era of low taxation. Federal income tax had not yet been made legal. Men like Carnegie and Rockefeller were hard pressed to find some use for their vast wealth. Both men gave regularly and generously to charity. Both became convinced by others that they would be wise to place their giving on a more orderly, systematic basis by establishing a foundation. Better, the foundation would continue to function long after they died. Thus they would be creating a legacy that might make their name, wealth, and ethical values immortal.

Carnegie and Rockefeller's rational for a foundation has been considerably eroded over the years. Federal and state governments now impose high income taxes, as well as high estate or inheritance taxes. Local governments also heavily tax the land, buildings, and furnishings of the wealthy. By the 1930's, the formation of a foundation had become a way to avoid the payment of taxes.

The federal and state governments impose high inheritance taxes, yet those taxes produce relatively small amounts of revenue, because most wealthy people engage in a practice known as "estate planning." There are three principal ways to avoid the payment of estate taxes. One is to set money aside in trust for wife or husband, children and grandchildren, all of whom receive the income from these trusts. In the United States, many billions of dollars are invested in trusts with financial institutions, law firms, and other agencies. The managing of trust accounts is a full-time, most lucrative occupation. No estate taxes are paid on trust funds until the last beneficiaries die.

The second method of avoiding taxation is a simple bequest to a nonprofit institution. A bequest can, for instance, be given to a church, a school, a university, a museum, a library, or a hospital. In a recent year the American Cancer Society received more than $24 million in bequests. The money, if accepted, must be used as the donor prescribes. Trinity College at Durham, North Carolina, accepted a large bequest on the condition that its name be changed to that of the donor. Today it is known as Duke University. Vast sums have been given for the care of pets. One eccentric gave several hundred thousand dollars to prove the existence of the soul, and, if possible, to photograph it leaving the body. The will was upheld in court and the terms carried out by researchers, although no soul was photographed.

The third way to avoid taxation is by creating a foundation. From a donor's standpoint, a foundation has certain advantages over a bequest. With a bequest, control of the money is gone. It is taken over, spent, or managed by the university, hospital, or whatever. The donor is remembered by a plaque on the door of a new building. With a foundation, however, control of the money or assets remains with the donor, his family, or those he specifies —perhaps forever. This is important, for donors do not usually give much cash to a foundation. They give assets, land, buildings, securities. If foundations did not exist, some of our largest corporations would be run by universities, hospitals, and other such institutions. It is difficult to imagine a university operating those twenty-six corporations left by Jesse Jones, or even one of them. The result would be to place a burden on the university and to cause intolerable interference with the management of the corporations.

In addition, very large estates of hundreds of millions or billions of dollars could hardly be wisely bequeathed. Which institutions would receive money? It seems better that the huge estates be kept intact through a foundation, which will spend the income wisely over a period of years.

Such reasoning hardly applies to the many thousands of smaller foundations. Why do they exist? Again one must think in terms of taxation. Perhaps, contrary to public belief, there is no need for a foundation to be created only upon the death of its founder. Many of our leading foundations were created by individuals in the prime of life. The Rockefeller Brothers Fund was created in 1940, when the five grandsons of John D. Rockefeller, Sr., were quite young. The Robert Wood Johnson fund was created thirty-two years before the Band Aid heir died.

In many cases, an industrialist, financier, or businessman will retire from these affairs and begin the active running of his foundation. Notable examples of this were Alfred P. Sloan, Charles F. Kettering, and Charles Steward Mott, whose foundations were based upon General Motors fortunes; William H. Danforth of the Purina Company; and W. K. Kellogg (cereal). In such instances, the foundations kept the donors active during retirement. They started the foundations off in the directions they wanted them to go.

A sort of "foundation racket" developed when the donor used the foundation as a tax dodge or even as a money-making opportunity. The "benefactor" would create a foundation and give over to it his assets, sometimes his corporation, even his home, its furnishings, and his art objects. The foundation would grant him and his family the use of these facilities during his lifetime and perhaps that of his heirs. The foundation might even pay the donor a salary and expenses as its officer or director. The advantage was obvious. The donor escaped taxation on the property and had the use of it, sometimes even deriving income from it.

There were many abuses. In one, the Public Health Foundation for Cancer and Blood Pressure Research, created by James H. Rand, Jr., of the Remington-Rand Corporation, the donor sold his Connecticut home to the foundation for $200,000 for use as a research center. He and his family continued to live in it, with the foundation paying Rand's household expenses, including the wages of servants. The foundation also invested $160,000 in a research laboratory in Florida that grew vegetables, which were consumed by Rand and his friends.

In California, Edward W. Carter, a director of the Irvine Foundation and a member of the Board of Regents of the University of California, gave the university a gift of $200,000 worth of stock. He presumably took a tax deduction for this act of generosity. Next, the university and Carter jointly purchased two acres of property graced by a lovely home and a Japanese-style garden, the university putting up $178,000 and Carter $75,000. The university received title to the garden, maintenance responsibilities, and title to the house after Carter's death. Carter received the house and land and the virtually exclusive use of the garden during his lifetime.

Some foundations became a thin mask by which donors, their families, and their business associates could maintain control of corporations, support relatives in opulence, and keep up baronial homes and gardens, while escaping taxation. Relatively little income from the foundation was spent for philanthropy, so that the foundation increased in wealth. In some cases, control of the foundation's assets made it possible for individuals to manipulate the security market for personal gain. In other cases, foundation directors used their money to pursue personal religious and political ideologies.

Foundations are the creatures of federal tax laws, and Congress has tried in recent years to eliminate the abuses through regulation. Foundations are now required to diversify their holdings and to divest themselves of excessive investments in a single corporation. There are provisions against "self-dealing" in which officers of a foundation manipulate assets for personal gain. Foundations are also required to spend a certain percentage of their income annually for philanthropic purposes, and they are expressly forbidden to engage in any form of political campaigning or governmental lobbying.

In 1969, Congress went even farther—some say too far—to discourage the formation of foundations. Congress sought to differentiate between private or family foundations and those described as "public-supported" or "operating." A public-supported foundation is one to which many people contribute, such as the National Foundation or the Kidney Foundation in the health field. An operating foundation is one with an avowed purpose, such as operating a school, hospital, or museum. The Longwood Foundation is an example.

Since 1969, the latter two types of foundations have been clearly favored over the private foundation. An individual can give up to 50 percent of his taxable income to a publicly supported or operating foundation and pay no taxes on it. That individual can also give property, land, stocks, and so on, and deduct its full market value from his taxable property. If the gift is made to a private foundation, however, only 20 percent of the taxable income is deductable, and property can be deducted only to the extent of the donor's original cost plus *one half* the appreciated value. As if this were not enough to discourage private foundations, Congress also imposed a 4 percent tax on the income foundations receive from their assets. The Ford Foundation paid over $4 million in taxes in a recent year.

Clearly, Congress has tried to discourage the formation of private foundations and to goad existing foundations into more dedicated philanthropy. This raises the final question. Should foundations exist at all? How useful are they? What service do they perform for the nation and the world?

Much of their natural, historic activity has been taken over by others. Direct outlays for the sick and needy, which the Carnegie and Rockefeller Foundations made for years, are now made by government and by thousands of organized charities such as the United Way, United Jewish Appeal, Catholic Charities, the Red Cross, the health charities. The federal government spends billions of dollars a year for education, health care, international aid, and scientific and medical research of great variety. The foundations, which once made large contributions to these fields, are now often redundancies—and likely to become more so if national health care and other social programs are adopted.

Foundations are a primary source of support today for private schools, universities, hospitals, and similar institutions. But is that support necessary? Many government programs support private institutions and do not interfere with their private decision-making processes. More to the point, when foundations give money to private institutions, they are acting as transfer agents. The money flows from donor to foundation to institution. It is argued that the money could just as well go from donor to university, or from donor to hospital, day-care center, or researcher.

In acting as a transfer agent, the foundation has little value except that it selects from among the possible recipients. It also lessens the donation by whatever its costs of operation are. If the fear exists that individuals would not make donations to private institutions—despite the fact that seventy-eight cents of every charity dollar comes from individuals—this could be encouraged by a change in tax laws that would allow individuals to deduct donations directly from their tax bill rather than from their income. The individual would then receive a much greater tax savings for acts of philanthropy.

The most convincing argument for the existence of foundations is that they can use their resources in imaginative and innovative ways as "seed money" to cope with the nation's and the world's problems. The idea is that foundations would employ, either on their staffs or as consultants, enough experts and scholars for an attack to be made on such problems as pollution, hunger, overpopulation, poverty, energy shortages, racism, and war. No foundation has the resources to solve such problems, but it could finance studies, research, and pilot programs that would illuminate possible solutions.

The best foundations already endeavor to do this, both by their own staff work and by supporting work in universities and other institutions. There have been some outstanding achievements financed by foundations. But the verdict of virtually every impartial student of foundations is that such activity, with few exceptions, has been timid and spasmodic at best. Most foundations do not even attempt it. Instead they remain conservative, safe, and unimaginative, acting as transfer agents for pet charities.

The concept that foundations can fulfill a vital, innovative role in American life remains more hope than fact.

Perhaps the best that can be said is that foundations are relatively new institutions. The oldest go back only to 1911. Most are much younger. With time and experience —perhaps some prodding—maybe they can come to a more useful purpose. A first and minimal step would be to require foundations to report in greater detail how they spend their money and to justify the expenditure. This would at least open them up to public scrutiny.

9

A Search for Reform

No one seriously suggests eliminating private, organized charity in America.

Organized charity, as distinct from personal acts of kindness or generosity, performs several vital functions in America. It is a way for the generosity of thousands of people to be combined and channeled into a useful endeavor, such as seeking a cure for a disease, feeding the hungry in a particular locality, providing recreation for a segment of the population, such as the young, elderly, or handicapped, and maintaining useful institutions, such as colleges, hospitals, museums, and libraries. Only the very wealthy would have much influence over these activities were it not for organized charities, which collect small donations and apply them to a collective purpose.

Organized charity may therefore be said to be a conduit for a mass of small contributions from the great majority of Americans who are thus given both personal satisfaction and the opportunity to obey religious injunctions to perform charitable acts.* It is also useful to society and its institutions because it gives many people the chance to participate in the affairs of eleemosynary organizations.

Organized charity serves a social and perhaps even political purpose in the United States. Every person who gives a dollar has at least some impact on the institution or cause receiving it. Most organizations benefit from this wide participation. Unregulated giving has also encouraged a wide variety of freedoms in the United States. Our freedom of religion may be due as much to the fact that Americans can give to any church or religion they desire as to the guarantees of the First Amendment. Anyone can start a church or even a whole religion as long as he or she can find people who will give money for the purpose.

The diversity of our educational system, particularly in higher education, results from the ability or willingness of people to give money to virtually anyone who has a system of education to offer. Indeed, much of the diversity in America results from our habits of giving and our lack of restrictions on how and to whom we give.

Philanthropy has a great impact on our political system. The First Amendment protects our rights of free speech, assembly, and press, but our gifts make them possible. Our giving supports just about every type of social, economic, and political opinion we can imagine—as well as a few we can't imagine and a lot we disagree with.

Our gifts are not just of money, but of our time and

*It has been said that one of the differences between Western religions and some of the more exotic Eastern religions is the emphasis Western religions place upon charity and good works as a path to immortality. Some of the Oriental religions place greater importance on an intellectual absence of striving or the desire to achieve personal relief from transmigration of the soul.

ourselves. We volunteer. From a survey in 1973, based upon personal interviews with a cross section of the population aged eighteen and over, the Gallup organization came to the conclusion that 38 million men and women had in the past done volunteer work for at least two hours a week. Another study by the Survey Research Center of the University of Michigan for the Commission on Private Philanthropy and Public Needs resulted in the estimate that each year heads of families (male and female) gave 2.7 billion hours of free time and wives gave 2.2 billion hours to religious or charitable organizations. Thirty-one percent of the family heads reported giving an average of 150 hours over the period of a year. In families where a wife was present, 42 percent said they gave to volunteer work free time averaging 128 hours a year.

Such levels of volunteerism boil down to massive participation by Americans in the affairs of the nation, its institutions, and its problems. Their participation is perhaps the finest example of democracy at work, and it is made possible in large measure by the existence of organized charities.

The elimination or severe restriction of organized charity in the United States would be unpopular with most Americans because the alternative would be unthinkable. The functions now being performed by private charity would have to be taken over by the government. The result would be a "1984"-type nightmare of regimentation, governmental paternalism, bureaucratic bumbling, and corruption. The United States would become less democratic and life would consist, even more than it does now, of a series of tax payments and forms to fill out. We would lose our individuality and simply become numbers to be processed through a computer. Our freedom of choice would be sacrificed to governmental efficiency,

133

except that the government would be less efficient because of the loss of competing services from private charities and because the innovation, imagination, and dedication a volunteer brings to his or her tasks would be gone.

Again, no one seriously suggests doing away with organized charity in America.

Yet dissatisfaction with the way charities operate in this country is considerable and growing. Indeed, our disenchantment with organized charity has its own history. The fund-raising success of Basil O'Connor and the National Foundation spawned many imitators. By the mid-1950's and early 1960's, Americans, particularly those living in the suburbs, were surfeited with charity appeals. Each major charity had a "month" proclaimed for its fund raising. Heart month was followed by cancer month, Christmas Seal and Easter Seal months, Red Cross month, and the Community Chest month until the whole calendar was taken up.

This may have sufficed for the major charities, but a host of other charities filled in the time with door-to-door solicitations. To have someone come to the door asking for a donation was at least a weekly occurrence in some localities. And the person at the door was not a total stranger, but a neighbor or friend who had volunteered—or, not uncommonly, been persuaded despite initial reluctance—to make the canvass. This was an oppressive form of fund raising, for it was embarrassing to refuse a friend or neighbor or to give just a small amount. The donor wondered what others had given and whether the solicitor-neighbor thought him a tightwad. In short, it was an intolerable invasion of the privacy of giving.

Subterfuges were developed to avoid these situations. A celebrated one was, "My husband gave at the office."

The statement couldn't very well be checked, and if the woman gave a dollar it looked like an act of extra generosity. This use of neighbor to solicit neighbor was done in by public resistance. Women refused to solicit in this manner. So many people stopped giving or gave such minimal amounts that use of the technique declined sharply because it didn't raise much money.

A parade of official and unofficial church, school, and youth groups was also engaged in raising funds. Churches began to use the pledge system, thereby tying up a portion of a family's charity dollar. The Salvation Army and Goodwill Industries solicited old clothes and worn-out articles. A visit to a shopping center meant a confrontation with persons selling raffle tickets or paper flowers or lapel buttons.

The mail was a disaster. The mailbox overflowed with duns for money addressed to "Householder" and bearing the cheap bulk-rate postage. The term "junk mail" came into use to describe it all. Charities were sending unordered and unwanted merchandise, then plaguing the recipient with bills and even threats for payment. And while opening the mail, the householder might be called to the telephone to hear an appeal for a donation from someone else. If, to escape, the person opened a newspaper, it might contain an announcement for a charity drive, a charity circus, or a charity football game. If the television set was flicked on, there was a reasonable chance of seeing a fund-raising telethon or hearing an impassioned appeal for money from a celebrity on a talk show. Nor was a movie theater a refuge. Intermissions were declared so that collection boxes could be passed among the audience to raise "desperately needed" funds.

It all became too much. The public cried out in outrage. Even the charities themselves realized that the goose lay-ing the golden egg was being killed. The public was sick of it.

An effort toward reform began. Indeed, the reform may be cited as evidence of democracy at work, for the public demanded some order out of the chaos. Congress rescinded the bulk-rate mailing privilege. Postage rates were increased sharply, and all mail was required to bear an address. This greatly increased the expense of large mailings. Many people began to throw out unread mail addressed to "Householder," even when it had an address. It became necessary for direct-mail fund raisers to have a full name and address and to pay first-class postage rates if there was to be any hope of success at all.

Many communities adopted or began to enforce anti-solicitation ordinances. Permits may have been given out routinely, no questions asked, but at least the solicitors had to go to the effort to get one or face arrest. This made some reduction in door-to-door solicitations.

The greatest reform was the thrust toward some form of consolidation of the various charity appeals, which had long been the goal of many people. It seemed far more sensible to have just one immense charity drive to which people could give generously. Then the contributions could be divided among the many charities. All the duplication of effort, as well as the harassment of the public, could end. The costs of fund raising could be drastically lowered. More of the charity dollar would go for charity.

Such a goal had been pursued for decades. There was the United Jewish Appeal and the National Conference of Catholic Charities. Perhaps the best known were the various Community Chests, a single appeal on behalf of many charities in a city.

The frequent success of many of these consolidated

drives should have encouraged other charities to join them, but there was opposition, particularly from well-known, successful charities. Some felt their identity would be lost in a consolidated drive. Those with well-known fund-raising techniques, such as the Christmas Seal or Easter Seal campaigns, felt they were better off on their own. Worse, some organizations felt they would lose their autonomy of action in a united appeal. The amount of money they could receive would be limited, and the way they spent it would be regulated. For some, joining a united campaign meant that those many organizations and individuals who profited from fund raising would lose money or go out of business entirely.

Despite the opposition, the drive toward unification of charity appeals was inexorable. The public clearly wanted it. Many cities tried to force it with legislation. Government agencies and business and industrial firms began to discourage and then to oppose solicitation among their employees. At the same time they favored united appeals and agreed to withhold an employee's pledge from his pay check, thus making payment easier. Gradually more charities joined the consolidation. Some insisted upon a separate identity for a while, so for a time many communities had the United Appeal–Red Cross drive. Some insisted on a separate campaign in addition to the united appeal. Even today, the Girl Scouts hold their cookie sale, although they are members of the United Way and receive funds from it.

From all of this the United Way has emerged as the nation's largest, most supported charity drive. Its growth has been phenomenal. In 1974, United Way campaigns were conducted in 2,240 cities, a figure that has been fairly constant since 1964. But the amount of money given to United Way has increased sharply, from $594.1 million in

1964 to just over $1 billion in 1974. That was the first time in history that an annual drive conducted by volunteers passed the billion-dollar mark.

These volunteers raised the money at a fund-raising cost of only 4.6 percent, well below that achieved by any other private charity. The United Way spends another 2.5 percent on social planning, 1.2 percent to develop allocation priorities, and 2.5 percent on management. Thus, almost 90 cents of every dollar given to the United Way goes to the member charities.

How much the individual member organization of the United Way spends for management and noncharitable purposes is confidential and not generally available to the public. The following breakdown of allocations was reported by United Way in 1974:

Boy Scouts of America	5.4%
Boys' Clubs of America	4.2%
Family Service, Nondenominational	6.7%
Girl Scouts of America	3.1%
Home Health Agency	3.0%
Hospitals	4.6%
Red Cross	14.6%
Salvation Army	4.7%
Settlement House/Neighborhood Center	5.8%
Urban League—Local	2.3%
YMCA	6.0%
YWCA	3.9%

The United Way is a tremendous undertaking. More than 20 million volunteers work at fund raising, allocations, planning, and direct service each year. More than 37 million individuals, groups, and corporations made contributions to United Way in 1974, and an estimated 34 million families were helped through the efforts of United Way organizations.

There are other consolidations of charities. The National Conference of Catholic Charities has a membership of more than five hundred social-service agencies and approximately five hundred institutions, which serve millions of people each year.

The Jewish Federations and Welfare Funds raise funds for 210 organizations and institutions. In 1974, they raised $670 million, a tremendous increase over the $365 million raised in 1973. The increase was in response to Israel's Yom Kippur War against Egypt, Syria, and other Arab countries. Of this $670 million, the United Jewish Appeal received $525 million for its human-needs programs in Israel and twenty-five other countries. Funds not allocated to UJA and other overseas agencies were used for educational, social, health, and vocational programs to enhance the quality of Jewish life in the United States. The magnitude of Jewish giving is indicated by the fact that, with a Jewish population in the United States of only a little over 6 million, UJA has since 1939 assisted 4 million Jews overseas, including Israel, and has allocated $3.7 billion for humanitarian programs.*

A number of major charities, particularly those in the health field, still engage in fund-raising drives. Churches

---

*In 1974, the largest amount spent on overseas programs by Jewish organizations was $445 million by the United Israel Appeal. It dwarfed all other international aid programs, including the $118 million spent by CARE and the $108 million spent by Catholic Relief Services. In addition, the American Jewish Joint Distribution Committee spent $27 million and Hadassah spent $20 million, both on overseas program. The tremendous sums raised, mostly from a small Jewish population, is a tribute to the concern and generosity of Jews. Many American Jews complain privately, however, that the tremendous appeals for donations and the pressure to give to Israel cause a considerable burden.

and religious organizations, schools, colleges and universities, overseas-aid funds, and tens of thousands of other organizations also make individual appeals for donations on a regular basis.

The dissatisfaction and downright suspicion of the public toward charities is based on more than the sheer number of drives for funds. The advertising and public-relations gimmickry have been growing worse since Basil O'Connor began to appeal to the gut emotions of contributors, and the techniques, once novel, have become drearily familiar. Americans are surfeited with celebrities begging for charity dollars, pictures of crippled children greeting the President at the White House, photos of starving children with big eyes peering from the pages of a magazine. For decades, we have heard and read of the horrors of various diseases, the need for funds to attack them, and the great work being done by researchers. We have been scared out of our wits repeatedly by tales of epidemics, listings of symptoms and danger signals, and warnings that each person or a member of his family is a potential victim. Every disease seems to be more prevalent than any other, worse in its effects, more horrible to contemplate, and more expensive to combat. Every cause seems more righteous, more needed to fend off pervasive foreign or domestic ideological menaces. We are asked to protect our children, educate our youth for a better tomorrow, care for the sick, needy, and elderly so often that one would think few Americans were left who were well enough and prosperous enough to donate.

It would seem, too, that charities have tried to part contributors from their money in every conceivable way (though probably not). We are barraged with appeals to our generosity, fears, love, protectiveness. We are told how we can deduct our contribution from our income tax.

We are told—are we ever!—how far a few cents or dollars can go to relieve suffering and how our gift will add up just to a pack of cigarettes or some other inconsequential luxury in our lives.

Yes, it has gotten a bit thin. It is not just that so much of it goes on, but that all of these appeals are first cousins to the advertising and sales pitches that saturate our lives on television and radio, in newspapers, and magazines, on signs and billboards. One can no more hide from a charity appeal than from any other form of advertising. And the distrust of advertising and the resistance to it spill over into charity giving. People suspect more and more that if a cause is a just one and the charity well run, this sort of high-pressure fund raising would not have to be used. Most churches, for example, raise a lot of money just by asking for it. They don't usually hire a Madison Avenue genius.

Many Americans have been turned off, too, by repeated revelations of charity frauds. This book has listed many of them—the use of foundations to avoid taxation, the bankrupting of charities by crooks, the misappropriation of funds, when as much as 90 percent of the proceeds are spent on fund raising, the wasteful management, the hiring of eight-year-old kids to sell candy under the guise of charity. The deliberate milking of the highly thought of Sister Kenny Foundation in the 1950's was a big shock to Americans. Things like that weren't supposed to happen to good causes.

The Disabled American Veterans was another big shock. During and after World War II, certainly up to the quagmire of the war in Vietnam, Americans respected veterans and veteran organizations. Above all, Americans felt a special debt of gratitude toward disabled veterans. If ever there was a charity with a natural appeal to American generosity, it was the DAV. It had a high visibility among charities. Its ident-o-tags were a fund-raising fixture. That it raised over $61 million from 1967 through 1971, as much as $20 million of that in 1971 alone, was not at all surprising.

What was shocking was that so little of that money went for any charitable purpose. As we have seen, use of the ident-o-tag was an expensive way to raise money, and while it enriched Abraham Koolish, it impoverished the DAV by consuming from 50 to 70 percent of the donations in fund-raising costs.

The DAV has also been victimized in other ways. One of its officers resigned after charges were aired that he used DAV funds to buy gift merchandise for DAV from his own company. The DAV rewarded him by keeping him on the payroll for two years after he resigned so that he could qualify for his pension.

The organization became involved in another odious fund-raising scheme when it became associated with an individual who was to solicit gifts of property from corporations. Half was to go to the individual, half to the DAV. Ultimately, the DAV earned $2 million from the scheme. Their fund raiser not only got another $2 million, which he was entitled to under the dubious contract, he also skimmed another million off the top that he didn't tell the DAV about.

The complaint about the DAV is not just that so much of its money was wasted on fund raising and fraud, but that it accomplishes so very little with what is left. Most of the alleged services of this Congressionally charted organization are duplications of those provided by the Veterans Administration. Most of its funds, including $1 million raised in dues from its 300,000 members, go for a national publication, a national convention, management costs, and expenses. It has abused the trust put in it by Congress and the American people.

An even greater shock, if possible, has been Boys Town, the celebrated facility for homeless boys in Nebraska. It was the subject of a movie starring Spencer Tracy, which is still remembered as a gripping tear-jerker. On the basis of its celebrity status, the affections of the American people, and aggressive fund raising, Boys Town has raised millions of dollars a year for decades. It has recently been revealed that Boys Town has so much money that it cannot begin to spend it all, particularly since its population of homeless boys has dwindled and its educational program lacks appeal to ghetto and minority youth. Nevertheless, the money keeps pouring in.

Sister Kenny, Disabled Veterans, Boys Town. If there are problems with such sacrosanct charities, no wonder suspicions are raised about lesser known ones.

The scandals and evidence of fraud, the dissatisfaction with the number of appeals and with the way money is raised have all led to a questioning of the purposes of charities and how they spend their money. People are now beginning to ask before they give about a charity's fund-raising costs, management expenses, and programs. How much goes for research or community service? How much actually benefits the sick and needy and handicapped and hungry in whose name the funds were solicited?

The answers are turning out to be elusive. For many charities the answers are nonexistent. If a citizen writes to ask for an annual report and financial statement, many charities will not reply at all and many others will send only fund-raising and promotional brochures. When the required data are submitted, much of them are unaudited and subject to several interpretations. Only relatively few of the best-known charities provide understandable, audited financial reports. As mentioned previously, it is difficult to obtain information even on organizations that belong to United Way or are listed by the Agency for International Development.

There is a growing body of opinion that something ought to be done to protect both the contributors and recipients of organized charity from those who, in the name of charity, engage in self-serving inefficiency, mismanagement, and even fraud. The problem is what to do that does not inhibit the worthwhile purposes and benefits of private charity in America. No one wants to reduce the level of giving in the United States or to eliminate the many contributions of private charity. In short, no one wants to create a monolithic big-brother government that leaves no room for organized private generosity. Above all, no one wants government to decide what charity is and whether people ought to contribute to it.

A beginning of reform, one apparently already started, is simple recognition that everything done in the name of charity is not necessarily charitable and everything done in the name of religion is not necessarily religious. There is a charity racket. Fraud does exist. People are bilked of millions of dollars a year. Some of the recipients of the charity dollar are more alleged than real, and may turn out to be merely a fat-cat fund raiser sunning himself in the Caribbean and buying his girl friend another mink coat. Our faith in charity and fund raisers has sometimes been misplaced. Everything done in the name of charity is not sacrosanct. Everyone who criticizes a charity is not a cynical tightwad, and at least some who give to charities are more foolish than generous.

One way to expose and eliminate the charity rackets is through government regulation. Acting on the information uncovered by his subcommittee, Senator Mondale has introduced the Truth in Contributions Act. This measure would require each tax-exempt charity to disclose to the Internal Revenue Service how much money went to program efforts, to administrative costs, and to fund raising. This information would be readily available to the public, and a shorter version of the information would have to be included in every mailing or solicitation of funds. The IRS would be charged to develop a reporting form that offers clear, concise, and uniform information about a charity. Perhaps the most controversial portion of the bill is the requirement that a charity spend 50 percent of its funds for a charitable program or lose its tax-exempt status. A newly organized charity would have four years to comply with this provision. At this writing, Congress has taken no action on Mr. Mondale's bill.

This sort of regulation does not have to come from the government. The charity industry could engage in a greater degree of self-regulation. The situation cries aloud, at a minimum, for some kind of central clearinghouse of information on charities that an individual can contact for accurate facts on finances and programs.

It is inherently ridiculous that an American citizen cannot find out from an independent governmental or other official source how much money a charity raised in a given year and how it spent its money. Under the penalty of law or disapproval of its fund-raising efforts, the charity should be compelled to provide accurate information, audited, if necessary, that is understandable to the average citizen and uniform for similar types of organizations. Providing such information would not be an undue invasion of an organization's privacy and would impose little hardship on anyone except fraudulent or inefficient operators.

It would not be unreasonable to ask that an organization soliciting funds or selling merchandise in the name of charity be required to register and make a report of its activities. Some exceptions might have to be made for small church and school fund-raising activities, such as bazaars, bake sales, and membership drives, but registration of organizations raising over a certain dollar amount or operating in interstate commerce is certainly feasible.

The amazing thing is that some central or regional clearinghouse for registration and information does not now exist. The four-person staff of the Better Business Bureau is inadequate, despite its dedication. The National Information Bureau does not fill the need, either. The Internal Revenue Service lacks both the statutory power and the personnel to police the charity rackets.

The great bugaboo of charity regulation is that government licensing would constitute interference, and would bring the government into the business of defining what a religion is or what a charity is and what they ought to do, and of measuring how well they do it. Such interference would probably violate the First Amendment rights to free religious worship, speech, and assembly. However, the requirement that a charity simply register and then open itself to public scrutiny by providing accurate information on its activities would constitute neither restraint nor interference on its activities, and would give the individual citizen a chance to find out about a charity and make a personal judgment of its value. The news media would then be able to report accurately on charities that reveal excessive fund-raising and management expenses, as well as those that fail to engage in any meaningful charity work.

Such regulation would not punish or inconvenience legitimate charities. Those harmed would be the ones that ought to be harmed, the charity rackets, as well as those who fail to report or who commit fraud. Existing laws against fraud would probably be sufficient to punish the crooks.

Reputable charities ought to welcome the public's awareness of their efficient management and many accomplishments, as well as the lifting of the aura of suspicion that now pervades the charity field.

There have been too many charity rackets. The trust the American people have placed in charitable causes and in those who collect money in the name of charity has been abused. The American people have been and are being victimized in a particularly cruel and cynical way. It now seems inevitable that more states and even the federal government will enact laws requiring the registration of charities and, it is hoped, the accurate reporting of financial data. Those private charities that solicit funds from the public should be open to public scrutiny. We should all demand it.

Index

INDEX

155

INDEX

INDEX

INDEX

INDEX